Samuel French Acting Edition

Bella: An American Tall Tale

by Kirsten Childs

SAMUELFRENCH.COM   SAMUELFRENCH.CO.UK

Copyright © 2019 by Kirsten Childs
All Rights Reserved

BELLA: AN AMERICAN TALL TALE is fully protected under the copyright laws of the United States of America, the British Commonwealth, including Canada, and all other countries of the Copyright Union. All rights, including professional and amateur stage productions, recitation, lecturing, public reading, motion picture, radio broadcasting, television and the rights of translation into foreign languages are strictly reserved.

ISBN 978-0-573-70737-7

www.SamuelFrench.com
www.SamuelFrench.co.uk

FOR PRODUCTION ENQUIRIES

UNITED STATES AND CANADA
Info@SamuelFrench.com
1-866-598-8449

UNITED KINGDOM AND EUROPE
Plays@SamuelFrench.co.uk
020-7255-4302

Each title is subject to availability from Samuel French, depending upon country of performance. Please be aware that *BELLA: AN AMERICAN TALL TALE* may not be licensed by Samuel French in your territory. Professional and amateur producers should contact the nearest Samuel French office or licensing partner to verify availability.

CAUTION: Professional and amateur producers are hereby warned that *BELLA: AN AMERICAN TALL TALE* is subject to a licensing fee. Publication of this play(s) does not imply availability for performance. Both amateurs and professionals considering a production are strongly advised to apply to Samuel French before starting rehearsals, advertising, or booking a theater. A licensing fee must be paid whether the title(s) is presented for charity or gain and whether or not admission is charged. Professional/Stock licensing fees are quoted upon application to Samuel French.

No one shall make any changes in this title(s) for the purpose of production. No part of this book may be reproduced, stored in a retrieval system, or transmitted in any form, by any means, now known or yet to be invented, including mechanical, electronic, photocopying, recording, videotaping, or otherwise, without the prior written permission of the publisher. No one shall upload this title(s), or part of this title(s), to any social media websites.

For all enquiries regarding motion picture, television, and other media rights, please contact Samuel French.

MUSIC USE NOTE

Licensees are solely responsible for obtaining formal written permission from copyright owners to use copyrighted music in the performance of this play and are strongly cautioned to do so. If no such permission is obtained by the licensee, then the licensee must use only original music that the licensee owns and controls. Licensees are solely responsible and liable for all music clearances and shall indemnify the copyright owners of the play(s) and their licensing agent, Samuel French, against any costs, expenses, losses and liabilities arising from the use of music by licensees. Please contact the appropriate music licensing authority in your territory for the rights to any incidental music.

IMPORTANT BILLING AND CREDIT REQUIREMENTS

If you have obtained performance rights to this title, please refer to your licensing agreement for important billing and credit requirements.

BELLA: AN AMERICAN TALL TALE was comissioned by Playwrights Horizons and was first produced by Playwrights Horizons in New York, New York on May 19, 2017. The performance was directed by Robert O'Hara, with sets by Clint Ramos, costumes by Dede M. Ayite, lights by Japhy Weideman, sound by Lindsay Jones, projections by Jeff Sugg, and hair, wig, and make-up by Dave Bova and J. Jared Janas. The orchestrations were by Daryl Waters. The production stage manager was Erin Gioia Albrecht. The cast was as follows:

BELLA	Ashley D. Kelley
AUNT DINAH / IDA LOU SIMPSON	Marinda Anderson
DIEGO MORENO / CP CONYERS	Yurel Echezarreta
NATHANIEL BECKWORTH	Brandon Gill
GABRIEL CONYERS / SCOOTER	Olli Haaskivi
SNAGGLETOOTH HOSKINS / BONNY JOHNNY	Kevin Massey
MR. DINWIDDIE / SCUMBUCKET	Jo'Nathan Michael
MISS CABBAGESTALK / MAMA	Kenita R. Miller
TOMMIE HAW / SKEETER	Paolo Montalban
MRS. DINWIDDIE / NURSE	Gabrielle Reyes
ALOYSIUS T. HUNNICUT	Britton Smith
GRANDMA / SPIRIT OF THE BOOTY	NaTasha Yvette Williams

CHARACTERS

BELLA
AUNT DINAH / IDA LOU SIMPSON
DIEGO MORENO / CP CONYERS
NATHANIEL BECKWORTH
GABRIEL CONYERS / SCOOTER
SNAGGLETOOTH HOSKINS / BONNY JOHNNY
MR. DINWIDDIE / SCUMBUCKET
MISS CABBAGESTALK / MAMA
TOMMIE HAW / SKEETER
MRS. DINWIDDIE
ALOYSIUS T. HUNNICUT
GRANDMA / SPIRIT OF THE BOOTY

Please contact your licensing representative for a more in depth potential doubling scheme, should you require.

SETTING

Mississippi and the Old West

TIME

Late Nineteenth Century

AUTHOR'S NOTES

This American tall tale is a big-assed lie created to point out outrageous American home truths. So please, my dear actors, put your booty in it.

ACT I

Scene One

[MUSIC NO. 00 "OVERTURE"]

(A large scrim is illuminated, showing the title of the book – The Thrilling Adventures of Tupelo Bella *– in nineteenth century font. As the overture comes to an end, the silhouette of a woman with a large, voluptuous behind can be seen. Lights reveal she is* **ISABELLA "BELLA" PATTERSON,** *a young woman of late nineteenth century America.)*

[MUSIC NO. 01: "BIG BOOTY TUPELO GAL"]

ALL PASSENGERS.
    OOOO...
BELLA.
    HISTORY IS THE TALL TALE
    THAT YOU LEARN
    FROM THE BOOK OF THE SCHOLAR
    BUT THERE'S ANOTHER HISTORY
    YOU CAN LEARN
    FROM THE TALE THAT IS TALLER
    AND WILDER AND LOUDER
    MORE FULL OF COLOR, TOO...
    LIKE THIS TALE THAT'S ONE HUNDRED AND TEN
        PERCENT
    ABSOLUTELY TRUE

BELLA. And now, ladies and gentlemen, boys and girls, a story so incredible, you simply will not believe your ears and eyes. It is not for the faint of heart, the narrow of mind, or the thin of skin. For this is the legend of the Big Booty Gal. She was a Wild West figure with a Wild West figure, and her story starts around 1877, on a journey that was a true locomotion of hot steam and cool dreams.

*(The sounds of a jangling bell and a train whistle. A train **CONDUCTOR** yells.)*

CONDUCTOR.	**1 FEMALE PASSENGER.**
All aboard the Southwest Odyssey, departing Saint Louis, Missouri at 2 p.m. sharp.	WHOO! WHOO! WHOO!

*(**BELLA** steps into the vibrant and colorful interior of a nineteenth century train and scurries to her train seat. A porter, **NATHANIEL**, enters with **BELLA**'s traveling valise, stows it for her.)*

NATHANIEL. Here you are, young lady. Your ticket say you're comin' from Mississippi, goin' all the way to New Mexico – hoo whee, that's a fur piece.

BELLA. Yes sir, indeed it is.

CONDUCTOR. All aboard, all aboard.

NATHANIEL. Listen here, Miss –

BELLA.	**2 FEMALE PASSENGERS.**
Patterson. Miss Isabella Patterson. But bein' as we're friends, you can just call me Bella.	WHOO! WHOO! WHOO!

NATHANIEL. This ticket say Isabella Johnson.

BELLA. It do? – Oh yeah, it do, what am I sayin', I'm Isabella Johnson. I got a wild imagination, you see, and sometimes I just like to make up things, like names. But that's my real name right there, Miss Isabella Jenkins.

2 FEMALE PASSENGERS. WHOO! WHOO! WHOO!

NATHANIEL. Johnson.

BELLA. Johnson.

NATHANIEL. Okay, well let me give you a little tip, Miss Isabella Johnson – stay right in this car – don't even peek your head out of it – 'cause they got rough customers on this train, and they gonna get even rougher the further west we go.

2 FEMALE PASSENGERS. WHOO!

WHOO! WHOO!

WHOO!

BELLA. Thank you, sir, now let me give *you* a little tip.

3 FEMALE PASSENGERS. WHOO! WHOO! WHOO!

(A wry eye cocked at the paltry tip.)

NATHANIEL. Thank you, Miss Johnson.

(He exits.)

BELLA. Bella.

MALE PASSENGERS.
SHE WAS A MISSISSIPPI GAL, DON'CHA KNOW
TAKIN' A JOURNEY FROM TUPELO

FEMALE PASSENGERS.
WHOO! WHOO!

WHOO! WHOO!

MALE PASSENGERS.	**FEMALE PASSENGERS.**
OFF TO SEE HER MAN IN NEW MEXICO	WHOO! WHOO!

ALL.
BIG BOOTY TUPELO GAL

(**BELLA** *stands up to get a letter out of her valise,* **MALE PASSENGERS** *enter the train and gape at her body, focusing on her behind.*)

FEMALE PASSENGERS.	**PASSENGERS.**
ALL OF HER STACKED PROPORTIONS	WHOO!
MAKE A GROWN MAN SCREAM	WHOO!
SHE CAUSE YOUR GLASSES TO	WHOO!
FOG AND STEAM	WHOO!
THAT GAL WAS EV'RY	WHOO!
BUFFALO SOLDIER'S DREAM	WHOO!

BELLA.
BIG BOOTY TUPELO GAL!
PASSENGERS.
BIG BOOTY TUPELO GAL!

BELLA.	**FEMALE PASSENGERS.**
BIG BOOTY TUPELO GAL!	WHOO! WHOO!

MALE PASSENGERS.
HAVE MERCY!

BELLA	**FEMALE PASSENGERS.**
BIG BOOTY TUPELO GAL!	WHOO! WHOO!

MALE PASSENGERS.
HAVE, HAVE MERCY! HAVE MERCY! HAVE MERCY! HAVE MER – HAVE MER –

(*A prim woman,* **MISS CABBAGESTALK**, *enters the train car followed by a baggage laden* **NATHANIEL**. *Outraged, she scolds the male passengers.*)

MISS CABBAGESTALK. Gentlemen. Pop those eyes back into your heads, and return to your seats. Immediately.

(**MALE PASSENGERS** *exit.*)

NATHANIEL. Miss Johnson, this is Miss Cabbagestalk –

MALE PASSENGERS. WHOO! WHOO!

MISS CABBAGESTALK. Be careful with that valise, porter. I will not tip for inferior service.

MALE PASSENGERS. WHOO! WHOO!

NATHANIEL. I'm gonna seat you two gals together so I can watch over you better.

MALE PASSENGERS. WHOO! WHOO!

MISS CABBAGESTALK. I am perfectly capable of watching over myself, thank you very much!

NATHANIEL. *(Exiting.)* Yes, Miss Cabbagestalk.

MISS CABBAGESTALK. Hmph! You're certainly not a little girl, are you?

BELLA. No, ma'am.

(**MISS CABBAGESTALK** *sourly inspects* **BELLA**, *begrudgingly admitting.*)

MISS CABBAGESTALK.
SHE WAS A PROPER SOUTHERN LADY TO THE TIPS OF HER TOES
HER GLOVES WERE SPOTLESS AND HER HAIR WAS CURLED

(**BONNY JOHNNY RAKEHELL**, *a wealthy southern plantation owner being fanned by nervous servants, sits on his veranda gnashing his teeth as he reads then rips up a wanted poster with* **BELLA**'s *picture on it.*)

BONNY JOHNNY RAKEHELL.
AND TO ESCAPE HER PAST, THAT GAL RAN AWAY FAST
VENTURIN' OUT INTO THIS BIG BAD WORLD

BELLA.
>I GOT TO GO –

>*(A Buffalo Soldier, **ALOYSIUS**, appears at a frontier fort where he's stationed.)*

ALOYSIUS.
>OH BELLA, WHERE'D YOU GO?

BELLA.
>– WHERE TRUE LOVE WILL BE MINE –

ALOYSIUS.
>YOU WERE S'POSE TO BE MINE –

BELLA & ALOYSIUS.
>– AT THE END OF THE LINE

PASSENGERS.
>WHOO! WHOO!

MALE PASSENGERS.	**PASSENGERS.**
HAVE MERCY!	WHOO!

PASSENGERS.
>NOW, WHEN SHE WORE HER BUSTLE
>THEY WOULD STOP AND STARE

BELLA.
>THAT AIN'T NO BUSTLE, THAT'S MY DERRIÈRE

MALE PASSENGERS.
>NO, NO, NO, NO, NO
>THAT IS GOD'S RESPONSE TO MY FERVENT PRAY'R!

PASSENGERS GROUP 1.
>BIG BOOTY TUPELO GAL!

PASSENGERS GROUP 2.
>BIG BOOTY TUPELO GAL!

ALL PASSENGERS.
>SOME FOLKS ARE SCANDALIZED BY THE FAME OF HER
>SOME PEOPLE FAINT AT NAME OF HER
>BUT IT'S A MYSTERY WHAT BECAME OF HER
>BIG BOOTY TUPELO GAL!

PASSENGERS GROUP 1.	**PASSENGERS GROUP 2.**
HAVE MERCY	WHOO! WHOO!

PASSENGERS GROUP 3.
>BIG BOOTY TUPELO GAL!

PASSENGERS GROUP 1.   **PASSENGERS GROUP 2.**
>HAVE MERCY!   WHOO! WHOO!

PASSENGERS GROUP 3.
>BIG BOOTY TUPELO GAL!

PASSENGERS GROUP 1.   **PASSENGERS GROUP 2.**
>HAVE MERCY   WHOO! WHOO!

PASSENGERS GROUP 3.
>BIG BOOTY TUPELO GAL!

ALL.
>BIG BOOTY TUPELO GAL!

Scene Two

CONDUCTOR. Kirkwood, Missouri, Kirkwood, Missouri, last call for Kirkwood, Missouri.

BELLA. So far, so good, except for that one little slip up with the porter. *(Giggling.)* Kind of funny when you think about it. Mama always gettin' after me 'bout makin' up tall tales. But she the one come up with the biggest tale of all. The one 'bout my name...

> *(The chair **BELLA** sits in is now in her Tupelo home. **MAMA** and **GRANDMA** enter. **MAMA** paces, looks nervously out of the window.)*

MAMA. Don't talk to nobody, don't say where you from.

BELLA. Okay, Mama.

MAMA. What's your name?

BELLA. Bella Patterson.

MAMA. No, your name is Johnson, Bella Johnson. You got to forget the name Patterson.

GRANDMA. Why she got to forget who she is?

MAMA. Mama, I done told you why ten times already, plus you holdin' the reason right there in your hand.

> *(**GRANDMA** frowns at the wanted poster in her hands.)*

GRANDMA. What is this anyway?

MAMA. A wanted poster of Bella.

GRANDMA. Read it to me.

MAMA. I done read it to you already, it say they's a bounty out on her for a crime she committed against Bonny Johnny Rakehell –

GRANDMA. You mean that rich boy with the pretty face, wanna rape every gal in sight? Is he dead?

BELLA. No, Grandma.

GRANDMA. Now that's a crime.

MAMA. Talkin' like that don't do nobody no good.

GRANDMA. Speak for yourself.

MAMA. I will, if you let me. Bella, they sayin' you messed up Bonny Johnny real bad. Say when he came out that swamp his own mama couldn't recognize him –

GRANDMA. I hope he look like shit.

MAMA. Mama.

BELLA. It was an accident.

MAMA. Well, whatever happened, he out for revenge. That's why you got to remember your name is Johnson now.

BELLA. Isabella Johnson, that's my name, okay Mama.

GRANDMA. Ain't right a woman got to forget who she is, 'specially when she come from a long line of strong black women.

BELLA. Strong like you, huh, Grandma?

GRANDMA. And like that first Itty Bitty Gal with the big behind – what was her name?

MAMA. Mama. She ain't got no time to hear about your big booty woman.

BELLA. She didn't have no name, Grandma.

[MUSIC NO. 02 "THE LANGUAGE OF MY NOSE AND LIPS AND HAIR"]

GRANDMA. Yes she did, but they done tried to make us forget it.

ON A SHIP OF MISERY
SHE COME FAR ACROSS THE SEA
SHE WAS STOLEN FROM HER NATIVE LAND

MAMA. *(Irritated.)*

SHE DONE TOLD YOU THAT FIVE MINUTES AGO

BELLA.

OH MAMA, I DON'T CARE

GRANDMA.

SHE WAS FRIGHTENED, SHE WAS YOUNG
DIDN'T SPEAK NO FOREIGN TONGUE
BUT SHE QUICKLY LEARNED TO UNDERSTAND

MAMA.

IF I HAD A DIME FOR EV'RY TIME I HEAR THIS MESS
I BE A MILLIONAIRE

GRANDMA.
>THAT THE WAY SHE LIVED BEFORE
>WAS THE WAY SHE'D LIVE NO MORE
>HAD TO DO THINGS IN A NEW WAY, NOW

MAMA.
>I SURE HOPE SISTER GOT YOUR TRAIN TICKET

GRANDMA.
>OH SHE HAD TO LEARN REAL FAST

MAMA.
>WHAT'S TAKIN' HER SO LONG, BELLA?

GRANDMA.
>TO PRETEND SHE HAD NO PAST

BELLA.
>SHE BE HERE SOON, MAMA

GRANDMA
>BUT INSIDE SHE MADE A SOLEMN VOW
>INSIDE SHE MADE A SOLEMN VOW:
>
>YOU CAN PUT ME UP ON YOUR AUCTION BLOCK
>YOU CAN TALK TO ME IN YOUR FUNNY TALK
>YOU CAN CHANGE MY NAME
>YOU CAN CHANGE THE CLOTHES I WEAR
>BUT THERE IS ONE THING THAT YOU CAN'T ERASE
>THE MOTHERLAND, WRITTEN ON MY FACE
>THE LANGUAGE OF MY NOSE AND LIPS AND HAIR

Itty Bitty Gal never forgot who she was. And don't you forget who you are, neither...wait a minute, who are you?

>*(As **MAMA** bangs her head against the wall.)*

BELLA. I'm Bella, Grandma.

GRANDMA. Oh yeah, that's right, Bella, my sweet little grandbaby –

AUNT DINAH. *(Offstage.)*
>WHOO HOO HOO HOO HOO HOO

>*(**MAMA** peers anxiously through the window.)*

MAMA.
>DID YOU HEAR THAT?

GRANDMA.
>YES
>IT'S THE ITTY BITTY GAL COME TO SHOW US THE WAY
>NOW AIN'T THAT GOOD NEWS, MM HM –

MAMA. Shh.

AUNT DINAH. *(Offstage.)*
>WHOO HOO HOO HOO HOO HOO

GRANDMA.
>THAT'S THAT ITTY BITTY GAL, SHE 'BOUT TO SHOW US THE WAY, NOW AIN'T THAT –

BELLA.
>NO, GRANDMA, THAT'S AUNT DINAH

GRANDMA.
>WHO?

BELLA.
>AUNT DINAH

GRANDMA.
>WHO?

BELLA.
>AUNT DINAH

GRANDMA.
>WHO?

MAMA.
>YOUR OTHER DAUGHTER, MAMA – IT'S TIME TO GO

(Handing BELLA a cloak.) Put this cape over your head so it hide your face.

>*(She smuggles BELLA out to the wagon AUNT DINAH's driving, and hides her in it. MAMA and GRANDMA climb aboard and AUNT DINAH drives off.)*

You got a wagon, Sister.

>*(As AUNT DINAH hands a train ticket to MAMA.)*

AUNT DINAH. *(Cockily.)* Sister, you know me. Long as I got it, I'm gonna get it. I got a wagon *and* a train ticket, made out to Isabella Johnson.

MAMA. Praise Jesus.

AUNT DINAH. Jesus ain't had nothin' to do with this, unless you count Mister Boss Man shoutin' out his name at a certain moment late last night.

MAMA. That's what you had to do? Oh damn these mens to hell.

AUNT DINAH. Ain't so bad, Sister. I just close my eyes and think of Africa.

GRANDMA. Africa, where that Itty Bitty Gal with the big booty come from. She was special, she had the magic in her. She say –

BUT THERE IS ONE THING THAT YOU CAN'T ERASE
THE MOTHERLAND, WRITTEN ON MY FACE
THE LANGUAGE OF MY NOSE AND LIPS AND HAIR

MAMA. *(Mimicking her.)*

THE LANGUAGE OF MY NOSE AND LIPS AND HAIR
THE LANGUAGE OF MY NOSE AND LIPS AND HAIR –

If she got so much damn magic in her, how the hell she end up a slave?

AUNT DINAH. Sister –

MAMA. I'm tired of it. All day long, over and over and over again, I got to deal with this while my baby leavin' me...

(Breaking down.)

Leavin' me, all because she had no other choice but to – but to...

AUNT DINAH. *(Comforting her sister.)* What's done is done, Sister.

(Frowning in puzzlement.)

Although I got to say, I ain't never heard of nobody doin' it the way Bella done it. How in the world was that possible?

GRANDMA. *(Exasperated.)* The magic of the Itty Bitty Gal done sprang up in her, I told y'all that ten times already. I got to remember everything.

*(***BELLA** *giggles.)*

MAMA. Hush up with that gigglin', we ain't there yet.

(A train station appears. A train is starting up.)

AUNT DINAH. But we close, see? Guntown Depot, there go the train.

*(They sneak **BELLA** out of the wagon, hand her a valise and her ticket.)*

MAMA. You gonna take that train up north to St. Louis.

AUNT DINAH. When you get up there, you look for a colored porter to help you get on that train west –

MAMA. She don't need no man to help her on the train –

AUNT DINAH. Them colored porters is good men, Sister, she be all right. You got all that?

BELLA. Take the train up to St. Louis, and look for a colored porter when I get there, yes ma'am.

*(**BELLA**, **GRANDMA**, and **AUNT DINAH** style **BELLA**'s hair, straighten her clothing.)*

MAMA. Now fix your hair and put on your travelin' gloves, just 'cause you runnin' away, don't mean you got to look raggedy.

BELLA. Yes, Mama.

MAMA. And baby, please remember that life is real – it's real, and it's hard. So try not to let your imagination run away with you all the time.

BELLA. I promise, Mama.

MAMA. What's your name?

BELLA. *(Dreamily.)* For now, it's Isabella Johnson. But soon it'll be Isabella Hunnicut.

MAMA. *(Aside, to **AUNT DINAH**.)* If that no account soldier boy really be on the up and up, which I suspicion he ain't.

GRANDMA. Everybody always tryin' to make us forget who we are. I say, make your memory so big, nobody ever forget.

BELLA. Bye, Grandma –

GRANDMA. Who are you?

BELLA. Bella, Grandma.

GRANDMA. I don't know no Bella, get away from me.

> (**BELLA** *goes to hug* **GRANDMA** *who fearfully pushes her away.*)

I said, get away from me.

> (*As* **MAMA** *puts her arm around* **GRANDMA**.)

MAMA. *(To a hurt and sad* **BELLA**.*)* Grandma just playin' with you, honey chile. Ain't you, Mama? Bella wanna know what the Itty Bitty Gal say. Tell her. She say,
YOU CAN PUT ME UP ON YOUR AUCTION BLOCK...

GRANDMA.
YOU CAN TALK TO ME IN YOUR FUNNY TALK

> (*As* **BELLA** *steps into the northbound train and waves to them.*)

GRANDMA, MAMA, AUNT DINAH & BELLA.
YOU CAN CHANGE MY NAME
YOU CAN CHANGE THE CLOTHES I WEAR
BUT THERE IS ONE THING THAT YOU CAN'T ERASE
THE MOTHERLAND, WRITTEN ON MY FACE

GRANDMA.
THE LANGUAGE OF MY NOSE AND LIPS AND HAIR

MAMA, AUNT DINAH & BELLA.
THE LANGUAGE OF MY NOSE AND LIPS AND HAIR

GRANDMA, MAMA & AUNT DINAH.
THE LANGUAGE OF MY NOSE AND LIPS AND HAIR
THE LANGUAGE OF MY NOSE AND LIPS AND HAIR...

Scene Three

(**BELLA**'s *now back on the westbound St. Louis train. She has the wanted poster. She looks at it, giggles.*)

BELLA. Don't even look like me.

(**MISS CABBAGESTALK** *glares at her – whoops! she realizes she's spoken out loud. She stashes the poster back into her bag, then looks hopefully at* **MISS CABBAGESTALK**, *whose expression discourages conversation.* **BELLA** *swings her legs, then looks back and forth from the window to* **MISS CABBAGESTALK**. *Finally, she pulls out a letter. She hums as she reads the letter. The loudness of her humming increases until* **MISS CABBAGESTALK** *can no longer take it.*)

MISS CABBAGESTALK. Miss Johnson.

(*Pause.*)

Miss Johnson.

(*Pause.*)

Miss Johnson!

BELLA. Who? Oh yeah, Miss Johnson, that's me, Isabella Johnson, what you want?

MISS CABBAGESTALK. Please refrain from humming out loud.

BELLA. (*Politely.*) I'm sorry, I don't know how to hum 'less I do it out loud.

MISS CABBAGESTALK. Exactly.

BELLA. Oh Miss Cabbagestalk, I did not mean to disturb you, I know just what that's like – you sittin' down, mindin' your business, tryin' to think your thoughts and here come somebody, sit down right next to you, just as loud as they wanna be, just talk, talk, talk, talk, talk, make you 'bout to lose your mind, right?

BELLA. *(Loudly whispering.)* Don't you worry, now, I'ma be quiet as a mouse. Shh.

> *(She reads her letter. Something in it makes her chuckle softly. Then giggle. Then totally lose it, laughing a loud belly laugh.* **MISS CABBAGESTALK** *turns to her wearily.)*

MISS CABBAGESTALK. Something amusing you?

BELLA. Yes, it is. See, I left my mama's house back in Mississippi headin' to Fort Craig, New Mexico. Got a sweetheart out there – his name is Aloysius. He a member of the Ninth Cavalry – you know, the Buffalo Soldiers. Aloysius gonna be so surprised when I show up.

MISS CABBAGESTALK. He doesn't know you're coming?

BELLA. No, but I bet he want to see me. He been writing me all these letters, talkin' 'bout how he miss me – hey, you wanna read one?

MISS CABBAGESTALK. You would let a stranger read your private correspondence?

BELLA. We ain't strangers, Miss Cabbagestalk. We friends.

> *(As* **MISS CABBAGESTALK** *reads the letter,* **BELLA** *points out.)*

See, it say right here, To Miss Isabella – I'll let you read it yourself.

Scene Four

(**ALOYSIUS**, *in his US Cavalry outfit, sits at a desk, writing the letter by candlelight at an army barracks.*)

[MUSIC NO. 03 "PRIVATE HUNNICUT'S LETTER"]

ALOYSIUS. September third, eighteen seventy-seven. To Miss Isabella Patterson, Gum Tree Crossin', Tupelo Mississippi. Dear Isabella – no, no, no...

(*Scratches it out, then writes.*)

Dearest, dearest, dearest Bella...
HOW'S MY SHY DARLIN'? MY LITTLE FAWN?
DON'T BE MAD, BELLA, THAT I'M GONE
SOME RESPECT, AND SOME PAY, BELLA!
IT'S ALL IN MY PLAN!
I AM NOW AN ARMY FIGHTIN' MAN!

I'M ONLY TRYIN' TO GET US A PIECE OF THE PIE
NO SENSE IN LOOKIN' FOR IT SOMEWHERE UP IN THE SKY

THIRTEEN DOLLARS A MONTH, BELLA!
AIN'T NO CHICKEN FEED!
THAT, AND YOU, ARE ALL THAT I NEED

EV'RY DAY, I MARCH THROUGH FIELDS AND TOWNS AND FARMS
EV'RY NIGHT I FLY TO YOUR SWEET BROWN ARMS
I'M DREAMIN' I'M IN YOUR ARMS, ISABELLA
EV'RY NIGHT I AM SAFE IN YOUR ARMS!

GIVE A KISS TO YOUR GRAN'MA
YOUR BUSYBODY MAMA TOO
DON'T PAY HER NO ATTENTION NOW
YOU KNOW MY HEART IS TRUE
YOU'RE MY BUFFALO GAL, BELLA!
IT'S MEANT TO BE!
KEEP YOUR HOME FIRE HOT FOR ME!

LOVE, ALOYSIUS T. HUNNICUT,
YOUR BUFFALO SOLDIER BOY,
UNITED STATES COLORED TROOPS,
PRIVATE FIRST CLASS, NINTH CAVALRY

Scene Five

(With a disdainful sniff, **MISS CABBAGESTALK** *hands back* **ALOYSIUS***'s letter.)*

MISS CABBAGESTALK. His spelling is atrocious. And how come he calls you Miss Patterson?

BELLA. Just like you say, he don't know how to spell.

MISS CABBAGESTALK. Patterson doesn't sound anything like Johnson –

BELLA. Listen.

> *(Outside the train,* **DIEGO MORENO***, a Mexican cowboy, is strumming a guitar.)*
> **[MUSIC NO. 04 "¡QUIÉN FUERA LIMA! - PT. 1"*]**

DIEGO.
> COMING TO YOU FROM AFAR...
> STRUMMING MY LONELY GUITAR...
> I'M A CABALLERO!
> BOLD AND PROUD VAQUERO!
> AY AY AY, SOY CABALLERO
> AY AY AY, SOY UN VAQUERO
> AY AY AY AY

> *(***DIEGO*** continues chanting "Ay, ay, ay.")*

BELLA. That cowboy look just like a picture I got in my travel book.

> *(***MISS CABBAGESTALK*** reads the cover of an ornately gilded book* **BELLA** *pulls from her bag.)*

MISS CABBAGESTALK. *The Passenger's Companion* –

BELLA. *A Compendious Account of Picturesque Places and Objects of Interest For The Well-Seasoned Traveler.* "Ay, ay, ay" – lemme look that up, see what it means – here it is. "Ay, ay, ay." Made up words sung by incredibly

---

* Lyrics loosely adapted from two poems by Gustavo Adolfo Bécquer.

handsome Mexican cowboys who like to flirt with girls through train windows.

> *(Sticking her head out the window, waving.)*

Well, ay, ay, ay to you, too!

DIEGO.
AY AY AY AY AY AY AY AY AY AY!
AY AY AY AY AY! AY AY AY AY AY AY AY...

> **(MISS CABBAGESTALK** *yells out the window as she closes it, with a slam.)*

MISS CABBAGESTALK. Stop that noise!

BELLA. Miss Cabbagestalk, that's no way to behave.

MISS CABBAGESTALK. You're a fine one to talk. Traipsing after a man with no secure future and as if that weren't enough, now you're up here ay, ay, aying with some vagabond you don't even know.

BELLA. Ahh. Now I understand.

MISS CABBAGESTALK. What do you understand?

BELLA. Why you so dried up and bitter.

MISS CABBAGESTALK. Dried up and bitter – why, I never.

BELLA. I know. But don't you fret now – one day, love is gonna come up and grab you and turn you all around.

[MUSIC NO. 04A "¡QUIÉN FUERA LUNA! – PT. 2"]

MISS CABBAGESTALK. Love will never come up and grab me, Miss Johnson. I am a mail-order bride, on my way from Miss Tidwell's Academy For Colored Orphans, straight to a small mining town in Arizona, where I'm gonna be marrying a man with six children, probably working from sunup 'til sundown, and at the end of the day, I'll have to live with a husband who looks like this...

> *(She pulls a picture out of her purse.* **BELLA** *looks at it.)*

BELLA. Argghhhh! Miss Cabbagestalk, that man could never make you happy.

MISS CABBAGESTALK. Of course he could never make me happy. I'm incapable of happiness. Never been happy a day in my life…well, except for that time I tried out for Miss Tidwell's Colored Orphans Dancin' Fool Contest. Won first prize, you know. Yep, got a big old trophy, had the words "Gussie Mae Cabbagestalk Showed De Flo'!" engraved on it. I loved that trophy. Loved it right up until the day Zachariah Bracegirdle, the orphanage bully, snatched it out my hands and ran away, never to be seen again.

BELLA. That's terrible.

MISS CABBAGESTALK. That's life, Miss Johnson.

Scene Six

(Lighting change. **DIEGO***'s head pops up at the window.)*

[MUSIC NO. 04B "¡QUIÉN FUERA LUNA! - PT. 3"]

BELLA. Miss Cabbagestalk, that cowboy is climbin' in through the window!

DIEGO. ¡Madre de Dios! ¿Qué es lo que veo a través de la ventana de oportunidad?[*]

MISS CABBAGESTALK. You better get on outta here. You know darn well you don't have a train ticket.

DIEGO. ¡Muñequita dulce, quiero decir un poema a usted![**]
 ¡QUIÉN FUERA LUNA!

BELLA. *Ooh.* I think he *wooin'* me.

DIEGO.
 ¡QUIÉN FUERA BRISA!

MISS CABBAGESTALK. Don't be ridiculous!

DIEGO.
 ¡QUIÉN FUERA SOL!

MISS CABBAGESTALK. We don't speak Spanish, sir.

DIEGO.	**CHORUS.**
¡AY!	¡QUIÉN FUERA
IF I WERE MOONLIGHT, SILV'RY FLOWING MOONLIGHT	
IF I WERE BREEZES, GENTLY BLOWING BREEZES	LUNA! ¡QUIÉN FUERA
IF I WERE SUNSHINE, A BRIGHTLY GLOWING SUNSHINE	BRISA!

---

[*] Mother of God! What is this I see through the window of opportunity?
[**] Sweet little baby doll, I want to say a poem to you!

BELLA: AN AMERICAN TALL TALE

DIEGO.
    I'D GLOW AND I'D BLOW AND I'D FLOW INTO YOUR SOUL!
MISS CABBAGESTALK. I said, we don't speak Spanish!
DIEGO.
    IF I, I COULD BE THE MOONLIGHT!
    STEALING KISSES FROM YOUR CHEEK, SEÑORITA!

> (**MISS CABBAGESTALK** *shouts out, trying to draw the attention of an authority.*)

MISS CABBAGESTALK. Ticket, ticket, where's your ticket?
DIEGO.
    OH, AND IF I COULD BE THE BREEZES
    MY CARESS WOULD MAKE YOU WEAK, SEÑORITA
BELLA. You gonna hurt yourself.
MISS CABBAGESTALK. You simpleton.

DIEGO.	**CHORUS.**
YOU ARE THE PERFUME OF THE ROSES	AHH...
YOU ARE THE BLUSHING OF THE DAWN	AHH...
YOU ARE THE MYSTERY OF TWILIGHT	AHH...
YOU ARE THE BEAUTY OF THE SWAN	AHH...
YOU ARE THE FLOWER IN THE DESERT	AHH...
IN THE DESERT OF MY LIFE	AHH...
MY HEART WOULD NEVER BE WEARY	AHH...
IF YOU WOULD SAY YOU'LL BE MY WIFE!	AHH...
SEÑORITA, IF I, I COULD BE THE SUNSHINE!	
I'D GIVE YOU ALL THE WARMTH YOU SEEK, SEÑORITA!	

BELLA. What's he doin' now?
MISS CABBAGESTALK. It's obvious. He's dancing.

*(As **DIEGO** stomps and claps.)*

BELLA. That's some fancy footwork – what, what you want?

*(**DIEGO** gallantly offers his arm to **BELLA**.)*

DIEGO.
BAILA CONMIGO, BELLA MUJER!*

BELLA. Okay I'll try – whoa, wait a minute, now, I can't do that, that's too hard.

MISS CABBAGESTALK.
TOO HARD? IS THAT THE BEST YOU CAN DO? HAH!
I'M 'BOUT TO CAKEWALK ALL OVER YOU!

(Doing a mean cakewalk.)

NOW THIS IS CALLED "SETTIN' DE FLO'!"

BELLA.
YOU ARE DANCIN' TO BEAT THE BAND

MISS CABBAGESTALK.
THAT'S RIGHT, LOOK AT ME COWBOY
"AY AY AY" *THAT* – IF YA CAN!

*(As **DIEGO** swoops her up into his arms.)*

What are you doin' – put me down!

DIEGO.
BELLA BRUJA DE MAL HUMOR!**

BELLA. Miss Cabbagestalk, you smilin'!

MISS CABBAGESTALK. I am? I am!

*(As **DIEGO** and **MISS CABBAGESTALK** perform a pas de deux of Afro-Mexican ecstasy.)*

DIEGO.
VAMOS A VOLAR JUNTOS EN TU ESCOBA
EN TU ESCOBA DE ENCANTAMIENTO!***
AY!

---

* Dance with me, beautiful woman.
** Beautiful, cranky witch!
*** Let us fly together on your broomstick, on your broomstick of enchantment!

MISS CABBAGESTALK.
>AY!

DIEGO.
>AY!

MISS CABBAGESTALK.
>AY!

DIEGO.
>AY!

MISS CABBAGESTALK.
>AY!

DIEGO.
>AY!

MISS CABBAGESTALK.
>AY!
>AY!

	DIEGO.
	AY AY AY AY AY AY AY AY!
	CHORUS.
AY DANCE WITH YOU, AND I AM HAPPY	AHH...
MORE HAPPY THAN I'VE EVER BEEN	AHH...
DIEGO.	
POR FAVOR, BONITA SEÑORITA	AHH...
MAKE ME THE HAPPIEST OF MEN!	AHH...
BE MY ESPOSA HERMOSA	AHH...
MISS CABBAGESTALK.	
LUCKY CHANCE DONE	AHH...
SWOOPED DOWN LIKE A HAWK!	AHH...
DIEGO.	
VEN AQUÍ, MI CHICA GUAPA!	AHH...
MISS CABBAGESTALK.	
COME OVER HERE, AND	AHH...
TALK THAT PRETTY TALK!	AHH...

DIEGO.
>SEÑORITA, IF I COULD HEAR YOU SAY "TE AMO"
>LIVING LIFE WOULD NOT BE BLEAK, SEÑORITA!

MISS CABBAGESTALK.
>I HEAR THE SIGHS OF THE ANGELS
>IN THE LANGUAGE THAT YOU SPEAK

DIEGO.
>¡SEÑORITA!
>I WON'T GIVE UP MY STUBBORN STREAK, SEÑORITA!

>Me llamo Diego. Diego.

MISS CABBAGESTALK. Diego?

DIEGO. Sí, sí, me llamo Diego.

MISS CABBAGESTALK. Ohhh. Your name is Diego. I'm Gussie Mae.

DIEGO. Gussie Mae.

>*(He kisses her cheek.)*

MISS CABBAGESTALK.
>THAT SPANISH FELLA KISSED ME ON THE CHEEK!
>MY LEGS ARE SHAKIN' AND MY KNEES ARE WEAK!

>*(As **DIEGO** and **MISS CABBAGESTALK** exit through the window.)*

DIEGO.
>I'M GONNA OWN TU CORAZÓN
>INTO YOUR HEART I'M GONNA SNEAK, SEÑORITA

Scene Seven

(Lighting changes back to what it was before **DIEGO**'s *appearance at the window.* **BELLA** *is now talking to* **NATHANIEL**.*)*

BELLA. And they left right out that window, Mister Porter, ain't that romantic? Just go to show, when true love find you, you better grab onto it for all you're worth.

NATHANIEL. *(To himself, under his breath.)* How the devil do Miss Cabbagestalk be a mail order bride to Arizona and her ticket say Jefferson City, Missouri?

BELLA. What'd you say?

NATHANIEL. I said, sound mighty excitin', sorry I missed it.

BELLA. Don't worry, there's bound to be more adventures like that on this here train.

NATHANIEL. Well, you're sure entitled to your dreams, I reckon.

BELLA. Dreams. I ain't got no dreams,

[MUSIC NO. 05 "WHAT I WANT"]

less'n you countin' the ones when I'm sleepin', and I don't remember them.

NATHANIEL. Everybody got dreams, Bella.

BELLA. Not me.

NATHANIEL. Sure you do. I mean, well, what you want out of life?

BELLA. A stove.

NATHANIEL. A stove?

BELLA. A cast-iron stove.

NATHANIEL. You just want a cast-iron stove.

BELLA. *(Sucking her teeth.)* No, I don't want just any ol' cast-iron stove!

BELLA.
   I WANT A PHILO STEWART CAST-IRON COAL AND WOOD
      STOVE

NATHANIEL. *Oh.*

BELLA.
> WITH A FIRE CHAMBER AND A OVEN IN THE REAR
> THAT'S A STOVE WITH PROPER FLUES
> IT DON'T GIVE YOU COOKIN' BLUES
> AND A STEWART COAL AND WOOD STOVE –
> THAT IS WHAT I WANT!

NATHANIEL. Come on, Bella, I'm talking 'bout bigger things than stoves.

BELLA. Bigger than stoves? Hmm.
> MAYBE A FRENCH COMMODE
> WITH A CHINA WASHBOWL AND A PITCHER?

NATHANIEL. *(Under his breath.)* Oh, for heaven's sake.

BELLA.
> AND A DOUBLE WIDE ICE BOX MADE OF PINE OR OAK
> ONE OF THEM JOHN DEERE SULKY PLOWS
> AND THREE HORSES AND FOUR COWS
> AND A STEWART COAL AND WOOD STOVE –
> THAT IS WHAT I WANT
> THAT IS WHAT I WANT

That what you mean?

NATHANIEL. No. I don't mean big *things*, I mean big dreams, like peace between the races. World changin' dreams.

BELLA. Ohh, world changin' dreams. Okay, let me see…oh yeah.
> HERE'S A THOUGHT THAT REALLY GETS ME HUMMIN'

NATHANIEL. Uh-huh.

BELLA.
> EV'RY TIME I DO MY MENDIN' CHORES

NATHANIEL. Okay.

BELLA.
> A HOUSE THAT COME WITH PLUMBIN' INDOORS!

NATHANIEL. A house that come with plumbin'.

BELLA. That come with plumbin'
> INDOORS! THAT IS WHAT I WANT

Is that world changin'?

NATHANIEL. It's a fine dream, sure 'nuff.

BELLA. I got me a fine dream. And I can almost see it.
FROM THE MOMENT THAT I STEP INTO MY DREAM HOUSE
NATHANIEL. Walk me through it, gal.
BELLA.
WITH MY HUSBAND ALOYSIUS BY MY SIDE
NATHANIEL. Lucky man.
BELLA.
I'M GONNA CLAP MY HANDS AND LAUGH
'CAUSE I'LL HEAR MY BETTER HALF
SAY, "HERE'S YOUR STEWART COAL AND WOOD STOVE"
HIS VOICE ALL NONCHALANT
AND I'LL BE HAPPY
'CAUSE TO BE HAPPY IS WHAT I REALLY WANT

Scene Eight

NATHANIEL. Well, if good things come to good people, you bound to get what you want.

> (*As he exits,* **IDA LOU SIMPSON,** *a young woman with a babe in her arms, has heard the last part of their conversation.*)

IDA LOU. Good things don't always come to good people.

> (**BELLA** *points to* **IDA LOU**'s *baby.*)

BELLA. She looks pretty good to me.

IDA LOU. Ain't a she. My son, Matthew, Jr.

BELLA. Baby can't sleep?

IDA LOU. Walkin' up and down this aisle only thing stoppin' him from frettin'.

BELLA. Aww, so precious, can I hold him?

IDA LOU. Oh no, cain't nobody hold him but me or he scream, wake up this whole train –

BELLA. Come here, you little brown baby with sparklin' eyes.

> (*She takes the baby. He stops crying.*)

IDA LOU. I can't believe it – he don't do that with nobody.

BELLA. Not even his daddy?

IDA LOU. Died 'fore he could see him. We was savin' up to buy some land. Matthew – that's my husband – he always say, land's important, Ida Lou. You own you some land, Ida Lou, you got you some room to breathe. Said that up until the day they took his land and his breath away. The day they strung him up, and invited their friends and neighbors and children out on a bright noonday picnic to watch. My Matthew was guilty of three crimes. The crime of bein' uppity. The crime of believin' in the United States Constitution. And the crime of thinkin' that, for the south, the war would ever be over.

BELLA. I know 'bout how certain crimes only crimes for certain people.

IDA LOU. You must be headin' to Kansas too, then.

BELLA. Kansas?

[MUSIC NO. 06 "KANSAS BOUN'"]

*(Handing **BELLA** a flyer.)*

IDA LOU. Promised land for us colored folks, need a little peace and freedom from them nightriders houndin' us down south.

> *(**BELLA** reads, as an image of a "Ho for Kansas!" flyer can be seen on stage.)*

BELLA. Ho for Kansas, Brethren, Friends and Fellow Citizens.

IDA LOU. Land of milk and honey, Sister. Oh yeah.
ALL COLORED PEOPLE SOUTHERN BORN
LET DIXIELAND NOW BE FORSWORN!
THEM WHITE FOLKS THERE DON'T MIX WITH BROWN
THEY'LL STRING YOU UP, THEY'LL SHOOT YOU DOWN
START DUSTIN' OFF YOUR TRAV'LIN' GOWN
PACK UP YOUR SMILE AND LEAVE YOUR FROWN!
IT'S TIME TO BE KANSAS, KANSAS-BOUN'!

> *(**BELLA** and **IDA LOU** are out on the prairie, now part of a wagon train.)*

FOLKS MAD AS HELL THEY LOST THAT WAR

CHORUS.
MMM...

IDA LOU.
THEY WANT THINGS LIKE THEY WAS BEFORE

CHORUS.
MMM...

IDA LOU.	**CHORUS.**
NOW LATE AT NIGHT THEY WEAR A HOOD	MMM...
A ROBE OF WHITE THAT MEAN NO GOOD	MMM... MMM ...

IDA LOU.
> EYES FILLED WITH HATE, A HATE THAT BURN LIKE WOOD

CHORUS.
> MMM...

IDA LOU.	**CHORUS.**
THE CROSS THEY BEAR	MMM... MMM... MMM ...
WILL MAKE YOU KNOW	MMM... MMM... MMM ...
YOU SHOULD	
PREPARE TO BE KANSAS,	
KANSAS BOUN'!	

CHORUS.
> I'M BOUN' FOR KANSAS!

IDA LOU.	**CHORUS.**
I'M BOUN' FOR KANSAS!	I'M BOUN' FOR KANSAS!

MEN.
> NO MORE BIDIN' MY SWEET TIME

WOMEN.
> NO MORE HIDIN' FROM CRUEL CRIME

MEN.
> NO MORE TRYIN' TO GET BY

ALL.
> NO DENYIN' MY HEART'S CRY
> I'M KANSAS BOUN'!
> I'M KANSAS BOUN'!

(The people have arrived at a Kansas "town" comprised of dugouts built into a hill.)

IDA LOU.
> WHAT IS THIS I SEE BEFORE ME?
> PRIMITIVE DUGOUTS ON A DRY, DUSTY HILL!

MEN.
> STOVEPIPE STICKIN' OUT THE HARD GROUN'

WOMEN.
> ALL A-CRAWL WITH SNAKES AND SPIDERS

IDA LOU.
> THIS IS WHAT WE COME SO FAR FOR?
> THIS IS WHAT THE FUTURE LOOK LIKE?

(**BELLA** *takes* **IDA LOU**'s *baby.*)

BELLA.
THIS IS WHAT THE FUTURE LOOK LIKE
LIKE YOUR MAN

IDA LOU.
LIKE MY MAN...
MATTHEW...

(*The* **EXODUSTERS** *gather around a tree near a river.*)

Here, at this cottonwood tree, by the river, we start a new beginning as citizens of the great state of Kansas. Now let us all join hands, close our eyes and take a moment to give thanks for this glorious day.

ALL.
MMM... MMM... MMM... MMM... MMM...

IDA LOU & BELLA.	**CHORUS.**
WE READY NOW TO STAN' OUR GROUN'	I'M BOUN' FOR KANSAS!
WE RIGHT AND TIGHTLY KANSAS BOUN'	I'M BOUN' FOR KANSAS!
WE TUGGED HARD ON THEM HORSES' REINS	
NOW HERE WE ARE, FOR ALL OUR PAINS	KANSAS! KANSAS!
LET'S NOT REGRET THE THINGS WE DON'T YET KNOW	I'M BOUN' FOR KANSAS!
DON'T BE UPSET WE SHOUTED "WESTWARD HO!"	KANSAS! KANSAS! KANSAS! KANSAS!

IDA LOU.	**BELLA & CHORUS.**
'CAUSE WHETHER A BLESSIN' OR A CURSE	KANSAS! KANSAS!
WE'RE STAYIN' FOR BETTER OR FOR WORSE	KANSAS! KANSAS!
FOREVER, WE'RE KANSAS, KANSAS BOUN'	

IDA LOU.
    I'M BOUN' FOR KANSAS!
    KANSAS BOUN'!

BELLA.
    I'M BOUN' FOR KANSAS!
    I'M BOUN' FOR KANSAS!

Scene Nine

(The lights shift. **BELLA** *is back on the train, alone. She looks at her poster.)*

BELLA. I don't think Kansas far enough away from my troubles.

[MUSIC NO. 06A - BELLA / BONNY JOHNNY RAKEHILL - PREPRISE]

*(***BONNY JOHNNY*** *enters, snatching the poster.)*

BONNY JOHNNY. You're right about that, Bella Patterson.

BELLA. *(Fearfully.)* I ain't studyin' you, Bonny Johnny Rakehell.

BONNY JOHNNY. Oh yes, you are studyin' me. You're thinkin' about what's it's gonna be like when I catch up with you, 'cause nobody gets away with what you done to me.

BELLA. It was an accident.

BONNY JOHNNY. You had it in you all along to do that, why don't you just admit it?

BELLA. It doesn't matter anyway, you'll never find me, I done changed my name.

BONNY JOHNNY. You may have changed your name, but you're just as forgetful as that granny of yours, gal. And once you start callin' yourself Bella Patterson again, well...

(Waving the poster in her face.)

... This five thousand dollar reward here says, it'll just be a matter of time. Just a matter of time. Just a matter of time, ha ha ha ha ha ha ha ha ha ha ha.

(He tosses her the poster as he exits.)

BELLA. It was an accident, I tell you. An accident.

*(***NATHANIEL*** *enters.)*

NATHANIEL. Who had an accident?

(**BELLA** *quickly replaces the wanted poster with the "Ho for Kansas" flyer.*)

BELLA. Ida Lou, the lady with the baby.

NATHANIEL. The lady with the baby.

(**BELLA** *hands him the flyer.*)

BELLA. Yeah, see? She done dropped her flyer 'bout movin' to Kansas.

NATHANIEL. Oh, *that* lady with the baby.

BELLA. Did you know that the ground in Kansas is all a-crawl with snakes and spiders? They ain't gonna hurt her, will they?

NATHANIEL. Not a bit. *(Under his breath.)* ... Seein' as how she don't exist.

BELLA. Whatcha say?

NATHANIEL. I say, your lady with the baby ain't got to worry 'bout snakes and spiders in Kansas. 'Course now, if she come across a snappin' twig in the middle of the night, that's a whole other story.

BELLA. How so?

NATHANIEL. When it's night time out on the prairie, snappin' twigs can spook the cattle. I remember one time them longhorn steers got so crazy, we had to lasso a few of 'em 'fore they caused a stampede.

BELLA. Lasso 'em? You was a cowboy?

[MUSIC NO. 07 "GAL OVER YONDER"]

NATHANIEL. Back before I was a porter, I was the rooty-tootinest bull roper down Texas way. Hired on to drive cattle to places as far away as Calgary up there in Canada.

(*He and* **BELLA** *step out of the train into a western frontier cattle drive.*)

IT'S PURE HELL ON A CATTLE DRIVE
BUT, AS YOU CAN SEE, I'M STILL ALIVE, STILL ALIVE
FLASH FLOODS AND WILD STAMPEDES

> NEVER GOT MY SPIRIT DOWN
> I EARNED EV'RY BLASTED DIME
> AND I SPENT IT ALL IN RECORD TIME, RECORD TIME
> FIRST STOP WAS THE OL' SALOON, WHEN I HEADED INTO TOWN!
>
> SAID, HEY, HEY, LOOK OVER YONDER!
> SEE THE SASSY LITTLE GAL, YELLOW RIBBON ON HER!
> HOO WHEE! I GOT TO GO!
> SHE'S LOOKIN' MIGHTY PURTY IN HER DRESS OF CALICO!
> CALICO! CALICO!

The day Abe Lincoln said we were free, I headed west and never looked back.

NATHANIEL & COWBOYS.
> WHEN THE WAR ENDED SLAVERY
> I TRIED MY HAND AT COWBOY BRAVERY, BRAVERY
> 'CAUSE OUT THERE ON A CATTLE DRIVE, EV'RY MAN IS JUST A MAN

BELLA & COWGIRLS.
> IT'S PRACTIC'LLY ALL HARD KNOCKS
> AND YOUR HEART CAN GET AS HARD AS ROCKS, HARD AS ROCKS
> BUT SOMETIME YOU NEED SOMETHIN' SOFT
> GOTTA TAKE IT WHEN YOU CAN

NATHANIEL & COWBOYS.
> SAID:
> "HEY, HEY, GAL OVER YONDER
> ALL I WANNA KNOW IS, WHERE YOU'RE ABOUT TO WANDER"

BELLA & COWGIRLS.
> SHE SAID, "BOY, DONCHA KNOW?
> YOU'LL NEVER GRAB THE MOMENT, OR THE GAL BY BEIN' SLOW!
> BEIN' SLOW! BEIN' SLOW!"

NATHANIEL & COWBOYS.
> COME A KI-YI-YIPPEE

BELLA & COWGIRLS.
> COME A KI-YI-YIPPEE

NATHANIEL & COWBOYS.
>COME A YIP-KI-YAPPEE

BELLA & COWGIRLS.
>COME A TIP-TOE-TAPPY

NATHANIEL & COWBOYS.
>COME A KI-YI-YIP, PUCKER UP THAT LIP, AND SAY
>COME A KI-YIPPEE-YAY!

BELLA & COWGIRLS.
>COME A KI-YIPPEE-YAY! COME A KI-YIPPEE-YAY!
>COME A KI! YI-YIPPEE-YI-YAY!

>>(**NATHANIEL** *square dances with* **BELLA**.)

NATHANIEL.
>WELL, NOW!

NATHANIEL & COWBOYS.
>CHASSÉ LEFT!

BELLA & COWGIRLS.
>CHASSÉ RIGHT!
>WE GONNA DO-SI-DO!

NATHANIEL & COWBOYS.
>WE GONNA DANCE ALL NIGHT!
>SWING YOUR PARTNER!

BELLA & COWGIRLS.
>ALLEMANDE!

NATHANIEL.
>COME HERE LITTLE GAL, COME AND TAKE MY HAND
>MY HEART IS BEATIN' LIKE THUNDER
>I BEEN LOOKIN' IN YOUR EYES AND IT'S MAKIN' ME WONDER
>IF WE DOIN' MORE THAN A DANCE
>IF I KNEW THAT YOU WOULDN'T MIND MY ADVANCES, OH!
>I WOULD SHOW
>THAT I'M YOUR LOVE FOREVERLASTIN', YOUR LOVE FOREVERLASTIN'
>YOUR LOVE FOREVERLASTIN' BEAU

Scene Ten

(BELLA laughs and dances with NATHANIEL. They are now back on the train.)

BELLA.

COME A KI-YI-YIP!

(NATHANIEL swings her into a face-to-face position.)

NATHANIEL.

PUCKER UP THAT LIP AND –

(As BELLA gazes dreamily at him.)

You back yet?

BELLA. Hmm? *(Snapping out of it.)* Back from what?

NATHANIEL. From out on the wild frontier dancin' with the cowboys, oh yeah I got your number now, Miss Bella Johnson. You may want a stove, but that ain't all you want. You got an imagination that make you dream of glorious color in this dull and grey world.

BELLA. My imagination get me into trouble.

NATHANIEL. *(Leaning in.)* Ain't gonna be no trouble to kiss you, Miss Bella, no trouble at all –

(BELLA is mesmerized as he leans in, then remembers herself and pushes him away.)

BELLA. Only man gonna kiss me is my betrothed Aloysius when I get to the end of my journey.

NATHANIEL. Just remember sometime journeys end up different from where you expect.

(The train horn sounds, screeching of brakes. NATHANIEL looks out the window.)

BELLA. Why the train stop?

(NATHANIEL points out the window.)

NATHANIEL. Soldiers. Look like they searchin' for somebody.

BELLA. *(Wary.)* Searchin' for somebody?

NATHANIEL. *(Disapprovingly.)* Yeah, they got these Buffalo Soldier boys up here searchin' for Indians ain't that about a –

BELLA. Did you say Buffalo Soldiers?

> *(Running to the window, waving wildly.)*

Hey, y'all, yoo hoo.

> *(From offstage, catcalls, whistles and hoots.)*

OFFSTAGE SOLDIER 1. Do you see what I see, boys?

OFFSTAGE SOLDIER 2. Lord have mercy, I done died and gone to heaven!

BELLA. Say fellas, is Aloysius out there with you?

OFFSTAGE SOLDIER 1. Alo-whoo-shuss?

BELLA. Aloysius Hunnicut.

OFFSTAGE SOLDIER 2. Come on over here gal, I'll make sure you get your honey cut!

> *(Raucous laughter.* **NATHANIEL** *blocks* **BELLA.***)*

NATHANIEL. Where do you think you're goin'?

BELLA. To see Aloysius –

> *(***NATHANIEL** *takes her ticket.)*

NATHANIEL. Your ticket say New Mexico. If that boy in New Mexico, he's with the Ninth Cavalry. This here's the Tenth.

BELLA. I wanna see for myself –

NATHANIEL. All you gonna see out there is a bunch of men ain't been around a woman in a long time, go sit yourself back down –

BELLA. I don't want to, and you can't make me.

> *(***NATHANIEL** *sticks her ticket in his pocket.)*

NATHANIEL. And you can't get back on this train if you ain't got no ticket.

BELLA. That ain't fair.

NATHANIEL. You want to talk to somebody 'bout what's fair? Talk to them Indians them soldier boys is roundin' up out there. They ain't got no ticket neither, but damn if they don't have to get on a train and move to some godforsaken place called the Indian Territory. That colored men should be the ones forcin' them folks to leave their ancient homeland don't sit right with me. But you gonna sit right with me – you gonna sit right over there, yes you will. And I'll be back with your ticket when the train start movin'.

(He exits. **BELLA** *plops down on her seat and sulks, muttering.)*

BELLA. Who does that Mister Porter think he is, takin' my ticket, tryin' to kiss me –

[MUSIC NO. 09 "PRIVATE HUNNICUT'S LETTER – REPRISE"]

*(***ALOYSIUS** *enters.)*

But I didn't let him do it, Aloysius, I got about as much urge to kiss that man as I do a – a – a Chinese cowboy and everybody know ain't no such thing.

Scene Eleven

ALOYSIUS. Stay true blue to me, Bella. 'Cause
 EV'RY DAY, I MARCH THROUGH FIELDS AND TOWNS AND FARMS
 EV'RY NIGHT I FLY TO YOUR SWEET BROWN ARMS
 (He exits.)

BELLA. I'm flyin' to your arms too, Aloysius. I'll close my eyes and think of you, close my eyes and think of Aloysius...

> *(She's getting sleepy.)*

... Close my eyes and think of Africa...

[MUSIC NO. 10 "STAR SONG"]

> *(As she sinks into sleep, the American plains transform into the African Savannah. The sounds of African animals, African instruments. A **STAR** in the night sky twinkles brightly. **BELLA** opens her eyes.)*

STAR 1.
 WHOO HOO HOO HOO HOO HOO

BELLA. Aunt Dinah?

STAR 1.
 WHOO HOO HOO HOO HOO HOO

BELLA. Mama? Grandma?

> *(**BELLA** looks out at the landscape.)*

Africa. Land of my ancestors.

STAR 1.
 WHOO HOO HOO HOO HOO HOO

> *(**BELLA** leans out the window.)*

BELLA.
 ARE YOU THE ITTY BITTY GAL, COME TO SHOW ME THE WAY?

STAR 1.	STAR 2.	GROUP 1.	BELLA.
WHOO HOO			
HOO			
HOO			
HOO			
HOO			
	WHOO HOO		
	HOO		
	HOO		
	HOO		
	HOO		
WHOO HOO		HMM	Ooh, look,
HOO		HMM	the stars
HOO			are dancin'.
HOO			
HOO			
	WHOO HOO	HMM	
	HOO	HMM	
	HOO		
	HOO		
	HOO		

(**BELLA** *is now on the plains, watching in awe as the* **STARS** *begin to form a constellation.*)

GROUP 1.	GROUP 2.	GROUP 3.	GROUP 4.	BELLA.
WHOO		HMM	COME-A	
HOO		HMM	COME-	
HOO			A,	
HOO			KI-YIP-	
HOO			PEE-YI	
HOO				
	WHOO	HMM	YAY!	
	HOO	HMM		
	HOO			
	HOO			
	HOO			
	HOO			

GROUP 1.	GROUP 2.	GROUP 3.	GROUP 4.	BELLA.
WHOO		HMM	COME-A	
HOO		HMM	COME-	
HOO			A,	
HOO			KI-YIP-	
HOO			PEE-YI	
HOO				
	WHOO	HMM		WHAT
	HOO	HMM		
	HOO			
	HOO			
	HOO			
	HOO			
WHOO		HMM	YOU	IS THIS
HOO		HMM		STRANGE
HOO				
HOO				
HOO				
HOO				
	WHOO	HMM	COME-A	CREATION?
	HOO	HMM	COME-	
	HOO		A,	
	HOO		KI-YIP-	
	HOO		PEE-YI	
	HOO			
WHOO		HMM	YAY!	A
HOO		HMM		
HOO				
HOO				
HOO				
HOO				
	WHOO	HMM		COWBOY
	HOO	HMM		CON-
	HOO			STEL-
	HOO			LATION!
	HOO			
	HOO			

GROUP 1.	GROUP 2.	GROUP 3.	GROUP 4.	BELLA.
WHOO		HMM		
HOO		HMM		
HOO				
HOO				
HOO				
HOO				

*(The constellation has now completely formed. It is of a **COWBOY** who is shooting showers of brilliant shooting **STARS** from his double holster guns.)*

GROUP 1.	GROUP 2.	GROUP 3.	GROUP 4.	BELLA.
	WHOO	HMM	COME-A	
	HOO	HMM	COME-	
	HOO		A,	
	HOO		KI-YIP-	
	HOO		PEE-YI	
	HOO			
WHOO		HMM	YAY!	SHOOTING
HOO		HMM		STARS IN
HOO				THE
HOO				
HOO				
HOO				
	WHOO	HMM	COME-A	SKY!
	HOO	HMM	COME-	OH
	HOO		A,	
	HOO		KI-YIP-	
	HOO		PEE-YI	
	HOO			
WHOO		HMM	YAY EE	COWBOY,
HOO		HMM		COME
HOO				DOWN
HOO				FROM
HOO				ON
HOO				

GROUP 1.	GROUP 2.	GROUP 3.	GROUP 4.	BELLA.
WHOO	COME-	HMM	COME-A	HIGH!
HOO	A!	HMM	COME-A	
HOO				
HOO				
HOO				
HOO				

ALL STARS.
  KI-YI-YIP-PEE-YI-YAY!

Scene Twelve

[MUSIC NO. 11 "TOMMIE HAW - INTRO"]

(The **COWBOY** *steps out of his constellation form and saunters down from the sky. He is* **TOMMIE HAW**, *an Asian-American man wearing a diamond studded cowboy outfit and a gold plated ten gallon hat. He is strumming on a jeweled Chinese stringed instrument.)*

BELLA. That's the strangest lookin' guitar I ever seen.

TOMMIE. That's 'cause it ain't no guitar. It's a sanxian. From China, the land of mah ancestors. Mah people are the ones who built this railroad yer on, and they built it with their blood, sweat, and tears.

BELLA. Lord have mercy, you a Chinese cowboy.

TOMMIE. That's right, sugar pie. Ah'm Tommie Haw, a wealthy cattle baron, and the man of yer dreams.

[SONG NO. 11A "WAGON DRIVER'S SONG / TOMMIE HAW"*]

BELLA. You ain't the man of my dreams.

TOMMIE. This is a dream. And Ah'm a man.

BELLA. And what a man – but no, wait a minute. The man of my dreams is Aloysius T. Hunnicut.

TOMMIE. That's funny, 'cause Ah don't see no Aloysius T. Hunnicut 'round here.

BELLA. Well, I don't see no animals 'round here neither, mister wealthy cattle baron.

TOMMIE. Hold yer horses, lil' darlin' – in a minute you 'bout to see more than you ever imagined.

    IF YA WANT SOME FUN, HURRY DOWN TO TAPAN CITY
    THEY GOT SOME TASTY SWEET PERSIMMONS

---

*馬車夫之戀 ("Wagon Driver's Song") is a traditional folk song from Xinjiang, Northwest China

SWEET AS ALL THEM GALS WITH THEIR LONG AND SILKY
    PIGTAILS LOVELY EYES THAT SHINE LIKE DIAMONDS
IF YA WANT A HUSBAND, AIN'T NO NEED TO LOOK
    FURTHER
GIMME YER HAND AND YER MONEY, TOO
HOPE YER DOWRY'S BIG, MAYBE LIKE A MILLION DOLLARS
YOU KIN ALSO BRANG YER PURTY SISTER WITH YOU

    (Constellations of **ANIMALS** *appear and dance around* **TOMMIE**.*)*

ANIMALS.
WE LOVE YOU, TOMMIE HAW!
WE LOVE YOU, TOMMIE HAW!
WE LOVE YOU, TOMMIE HAW!

TOMMIE.
'COURSE YOU DO.
'CAUSE AH'M A RIP-ROARIN' BRONC-BUSTIN'
CHINESE-AMERICAN COWBOY

COW. *(Flirtatiously.)*
TOMMIE HAW, YA MOOVE ME!

TOMMIE.
AH AM A BONA FIDE, TAN YER HIDE
MAV'RICK RIDIN' RANCHER MAN

    (**COYOTES** *put their hands up in the air, waving them like they just don't care.*)

COYOTES.
ALL THE COYOTES SAY, "AH OOH, AH OOH!"

HORSE.
NOW, WERE YA BORN IN THE YEAR OF THE HORSE?

TOMMIE. *(Speaking in "***HORSE.***")*
NEIGH!

RAM.
WELL, WERE YA BORN IN THE YEAR OF THE RAM?

TOMMIE. *(Speaking in "***RAM.***")*
MAAAAA-YBE
BUT NOW THAT AH'M HERE
EV'RY STUBBORN MULE KNOWS WHO AH AM

MULE.
> HEE HAW! HEE HAW!

TOMMIE.

TOMMIE. That's right.	**ANIMALS.**
AH WAS A LITTLE BITTY ORPHAN	OOH
IN THE MININ' FIELDS OF CALIFORNIA	OOH

PARROT.
> HE'S A SOLE SURVIVOR, HAW!!!!

TOMMIE.	**ANIMALS.**
WHEN A RANCHER NAME OF THOMAS ORR	OOH
SAID, "BOY, AH'LL MAKE YER FUTURE BRIGHT"	OOH

OWL.
> HOO? HOO?

TOMMIE.
> AH SAID, THOMAS ORR!
> THAT MAN TREATED ME LIKE ONE OF HIS SONS

CAT.
> MEOW!

TOMMIE.
> HE GAVE ME LAND, HORSES, CATTLE, AND GUNS

DOG. *(Impressed.)*
> BOW WOW WOW WOW WOW, WOW, *WOW*

TOMMIE.
> AND HIS WIFE WAS THE LADY WHO
> TAUGHT ME HOW TO READ AND WRITE
> WHAT'S MAH NAME?

MULE.
> HEE HAW!

TOMMIE.
> CLOSE ENOUGH!

ANIMALS.
  TOMMIE HAW!

  TOMMIE HAW!

TOMMIE.
  AH START MAH CATTLE DRIVE
  EARLY IN SPRING
  TO PASS THE TIME
  AH TEACH MAH VARMINTS TO SING

TOMMIE & ANIMALS.
  WE GO: IF YA WANT SOME FUN, HURRY DOWN TO TAPAN CITY
  BUT TAKE A LITTLE TIME TO DANCE!

TOMMIE.
  SHAKE A HOOF, Y'ALL

ANIMALS.
  TOMMIE HAW

TOMMIE.
  HEY ANGUS BULL, LET'S DO THE HIGHLAND FLING

  (**TOMMIE** and **ANGUS BULL** dance a Highland fling.)

TOMMIE & ANGUS BULL.
  ONE TWO THREE A LEERIE!

ANIMALS.
  BRAW AND CHEERY
  TOMMIE HAW!

TOMMIE.
  MUSTANG SALLY LET'S DO A BUCK AND WING!

  (**MUSTANG SALLY** and **TOMMIE** do a buck dance.)

MUSTANG SALLY.
  TOMMIE HAW, CAN YA STEP?

TOMMIE.
  YA KNOW THE ANSWER IS YEP

TOMMIE & ANIMALS.
  WE GO
  IF YA WANT SOME FUN, HURRY DOWN TO TAPAN CITY

(Suddenly, the **STARS** *shine down like spotlights – it's time for* **TOMMIE** *to reveal his finest assets. As he lets it all hang out,* **BELLA** *demurely covers her eyes, leaving enough space to peek through her fingers.)*

TOMMIE.
AND MAYBE YOU'LL FIND TRUE ROMANCE!
OH HOW AH'M HOPIN' WHAT'S GON' HAPPEN

*(***TOMMIE** *flings his ten gallon hat at* **BELLA**, *who catches it with surprising ease for someone with covered eyes.)*

ANIMALS.
WHOOP

(Goodbye, bolero tie!)

TOMMIE.
IN TAPAN

ANIMALS.
WHOOP

(Ta ta, spurs!)

TOMMIE.
IS THAT I'LL SEE SOME MIGHTY FINE WIMMENS

ANIMALS.
SEE SOME FINE FINE WIMMENS

TOMMIE.
IF TAPAN GALS AIN'T GOT NO MONEY

(Ciao, chaps!)

ANIMALS.
WHOOP

TOMMIE.
WELL, SONNY

ANIMALS.
WHOOP

(Hasta la vista, boots!)

TOMMIE.
AH HOPE THEY'LL LET ME SAMPLE THEIR PERSIMMONS

ANIMALS.
> TASTIN' SWEETER THAN WINE
>> *(Arrivederci, pants!)*

TOMMIE.
> NOW, PEOPLE SAY DON'T WEAR YER HEART ON YER SLEEVE

ANIMALS.
> THAT'S WHAT THEY SAY!

TOMMIE.
> BUT AH SHOOT STRAIGHT, AND AH DON'T GIVE A DAMN

ANIMALS.
> COME ON TOMMIE, TELL US WHY?

*(**TOMMIE** has bumped and grinded down to his union suit. He rips it off to reveal diamond studded briefs with the word "Haw!" on them. As he saunters back up into the night sky.)*

TOMMIE.
> 'CAUSE AH'M A PLAIN SPEAKIN', SOUL MATE SEEKIN'
> HIGHLAND FLINGIN', BUCK AND WINGIN'
> SANXIAN STRUMMIN', FOLK SONG HUMMIN'
> MUSCLE BOUND, ALL AROUND
> RIP-SNORTIN', BRONC-BUSTIN'
> CHINESE-AMERICAN COWBOY!

*(Pinspot on **TOMMIE**'s face now in the middle of a heart-shaped **STAR**.)*

> THAT'S WHO AH AM!

ANIMALS.	**TOMMIE.**
TOMMIE HAW!	AH'M HEADIN' ABOVE, Y'ALL
	COME SHOW ME SOME LOVE, Y'ALL

*(The **STAR** winks out. Blackout.)*

Scene Thirteen

*(**BELLA** is asleep in her seat. **NATHANIEL** enters.)*

NATHANIEL. Bella, here's your ticket. Bella?

*(He slips the ticket into her purse. The wanted poster slips out. **NATHANIEL** reads it. **BELLA** starts thrashing in her sleep, crying out.)*

BELLA. I had no choice. You gotta believe me, Aloysius –

NATHANIEL. It's a dream, Bella, wake up –

BELLA. *(Fighting him.)* Why you wanna hurt me, Mister, I ain't nothin' to you, no, leave me alone –

(Waking up.)

Mister Porter. Thank goodness. Wait a minute, I ain't talkin' to you.

NATHANIEL. But I wanna talk to you. Miss Bella Patterson.

(He shows her the wanted poster.)

BELLA. You gonna turn me in?

NATHANIEL. I don't know yet. Tell me what's goin' on.

BELLA. Okay. Well, I know you can't imagine this, but I can be a bit impulsive at times.

NATHANIEL. No. You?

BELLA. Yeah. 'Specially when I see somethin' happenin' that ain't right. It's like this force come over me and it cause me to do...things. Things you wouldn't believe.

NATHANIEL. Try me.

BELLA. Back in Tupelo, it was real early one mornin', and I was walkin' down this road called the Natchez Trace, now I don't know why they call it a Trace, it's just a ol' road, and it was so pretty there, you know heaven must be like Tupelo –

*(Looking at **NATHANIEL**'s raised eyebrow.)*

– Anyway I was walkin' down the Trace and I came to a swamp. And in that swamp – oh, in that swamp –

NATHANIEL. Was a crocodile?

BELLA. Worse than a crocodile. It was a plantation owner. Mister John Beauregard Slaughterhouse, but everybody call him Bonny Johnny. Bonny Johnny big and tall and strong and he got in front of me. I begged him to let me pass by, but he wouldn't let me. And then...and then...

(She starts to cry. **NATHANIEL** *hugs her.)*

NATHANIEL. Damn that man to hell.

BELLA. You sound like my mama, that's what she say 'bout all men, but she wrong 'cause Aloysius ain't like that. And you ain't like that. You a nice man.

NATHANIEL. That you can still believe us fellas are good after what that bastard done to you.

BELLA. But that's just it, he ain't done nothin' to me, I was the one who trounced him.

*(***NATHANIEL*** waves the wanted poster.)*

NATHANIEL. I know that's what I'm s'pose to believe, but you just a itty bitty gal, Bella, ain't no way you coulda done that. It's a tall tale.

BELLA. Ain't no tall tale.

NATHANIEL. Yes it is, just like the lady who jumped out the window to marry the vagabond cowboy, the woman on her way to Kansas, and every story you done made up about everybody on this train. You didn't beat up that man, that's just your mind tryin' to escape what happened to you.

BELLA. It is?

NATHANIEL. Yes it is. Now what I want you to do is take a deep breath – come on now.

*(***BELLA*** takes a deep breath.)*

Now tell me what really happened.

BELLA. What really happened?

NATHANIEL. I swear I won't think no less of you for it.

BELLA. Okay. Well, you right. I didn't beat up Bonny Johnny.

NATHANIEL. See how easy that was?

BELLA. Yeah. I didn't beat up Bonny Johnny, 'cause it was my ancestor, the spirit of the Itty Bitty Gal with the big booty who done him in.

NATHANIEL. Bella.

BELLA.	**NATHANIEL.**
On a ship of misery, she come far across	Bella, Bella,
the sea, to rise up out of the swamp and	Bella, Bella,
cause a terrible accident to happen to	no, no,
that man.	

NATHANIEL. No –

BELLA. Yes.

NATHANIEL. No –

BELLA. Yes –

NATHANIEL. No, she didn't –

BELLA. Yes she did, and that's why he want revenge on me.

NATHANIEL. Maybe one day you'll trust me enough to tell me the truth –

(The train jolts violently.)

BELLA. What on earth was that?

Scene Fourteen

[MUSIC NO. 12 "A-BOUNCIN' BACK FROM ADVERSITY LEAD IN"]

(Spotlight on outlaw **SNAGGLETOOTH** *and his gang brandishing their guns outside the train.)*

SNAGGLETOOTH. We are the meanest, the cruelest, the most train-robbin'-est sonzabitches this side of the Mississippi River. The notorious Shoot the Spit Gang!

(Yelling out to the train.)

LISTEN UP, Y'ALL!
MY NAME IS SNAGGLETOOTH HOSKINS!
AND THESE HERE ARE MY BOYS!

Introduce yerselves, boys.

SKEETER. *(Twirling his guns.)*
I'M SKEETER!

SCOOTAH. *(Elegant bow.)*
I'M SCOOTAH!

SCALAWAG. *(Twitching nervously.)*
THEY CALL ME SCALAWAG

SCUMBUCKET. *(Popping flies into his mouth.)*
AND I'M SCUMBUCKET

SNAGGLETOOTH & HIS BOYS.
AND NOW IT IS TIME TO SHOOT THE SPIT, SO HARK!

(They all hark, spit, then fire their guns.)

BELLA. Ooh, that's disgustin'.

NATHANIEL. Shh. Come on, little gal...

(They head to the baggage car. **NATHANIEL** *pushes* **BELLA** *behind some boxes, motions for her to be quiet. In the front,* **SNAGGLETOOTH** *terrifies train passengers.)*

SNAGGLETOOTH. Well, well, well looky what we got here. The hard earned life savin's of an adorable elderly couple. Iff'n ya don't want me to give ya lead poisonin', old timers, ya better cough up the goods, 'cause I'm gonna rob this train and there ain't a damn thing your ass can do about it, heh, heh, heh, heh. Looks like a good haul boys. Time for me to check the baggage car.

> (**BELLA** *pops up from beind the boxes.*)

BELLA. *(In her original* **NARRATOR** *character.)*
AND WHAT HAPPENED NEXT HAS BEEN DISPUTED
BY EYEWITNESSES, HISTORY BUFFS
AND TALL TALERS EVERYWHERE

> (*Tapping* **SNAGGLETOOTH**, *who pulls a book out of his pocket to hawk.*)

BUT THIS HERE IS THE OFFICIAL VERSION
TAKEN FROM THE WILDLY POPULAR DIME STORE NOVEL
THE THRILLIN' ADVENTURES OF TUPELO BELLA
AVAILABLE IN THE LOBBY –
TWO FOR ONE, GET 'EM WHILE THEY LAST!

> (*She hides behind the boxes again.* **SNAGGLETOOTH** *resumes his outlaw persona. He sees* **NATHANIEL**.)

SNAGGLETOOTH. Well, well, well. Looky what we got here.

> (**NATHANIEL** *nervously faces down the train robber.*)

NATHANIEL. S-sir, this is f-federal property and y-you –

> (**SNAGGLETOOTH** *harks, spits, fires his gun.* **NATHANIEL** *drops to the floor, gasping.*)

– Trespassin'...

[MUSIC NO. 12A "A-BOUNCIN' BACK FROM ADVERSITY"]

> (*Outraged,* **BELLA** *jumps out of her hiding place.*)

BELLA. Ooh!

SNAGGLETOOTH. What the –
BELLA.
>WHY, YOU NO-GOOD, DIRTY LOW-DOWN
>TRAIN ROBBIN', PORTER SHOOTIN' VARMINT!
>YOU THRIVE ON FEAR?

SNAGGLETOOTH. Yeah.
BELLA.
>WELL, LISTEN HERE – I AIN'T AFRAID!

SNAGGLETOOTH. You ain't?
BELLA.
>NOPE!
>YOU MAY BE A SOUR LEMON
>BUT I'M FROM A LINE OF WOMEN
>WHO KNOW HOW TO TURN A LEMON INTO LEMONADE!!!

SNAGGLETOOTH. *(Chuckling.)* Well, look who's madder than a wet hen, heh, heh, heh, feisty little thing, you plum ticklin' ol' Snaggletooth to bits, hell if you ain't.
>THAT'S A MIGHTY FIERCE TONGUE-LASHIN', LITTLE GAL
>BUT I'M GONNA ROB THIS TRAIN
>AND THERE AIN'T A DAMN THING YOUR ASS CAN DO
>   ABOUT IT

BELLA. I wouldn't be too sure of that, Mister.

>*(She starts a shimmy of righteous indignation as she advances on **SNAGGLETOOTH**.)*

SNAGGLETOOTH. What's that yer doin'?
BELLA.
>YOU NEED MORE THAN A TONGUE LASHIN'
>SO I'M GIVIN' YOU A THRASHIN'
>LOOK OUT JACK, I'M A-BOUNCIN' BACK FROM ADVERSITY!

>*(She wallops **SNAGGLETOOTH** with her behind, he flies across the room.)*

SNAGGLETOOTH.
>OW.

>*(**BELLA** advances on him again.)*

BELLA.
> AND I WON'T ABIDE YOUR SNIV'LIN'
> WHEN I SET MY HIPS TO SWIV'LIN'
> LOOK OUT JACK, I'M A-BOUNCIN' BACK FROM ADVERSITY!
>
> *(She butts him to the left.)*
>
> I'M A-BOUNCIN' BACK!

SNAGGLETOOTH.
> ULP! OOF!
>
> *(**BELLA** butts him to the right.)*

BELLA.
> I'M A-BOUNCIN' BACK!

SNAGGLETOOTH.
> OUCH, OOH, AAACK!

BELLA.
> BETTER LOOK OUT JACK, I'M A-BOUNCIN' BACK FROM ADVERSITY!
>
> *(She butts him one last time. **SNAGGLETOOTH** flips over and lands on some baggage, now unconscious. **SCALAWAG** and **SCUMBUCKET** rush into the car. **BELLA** advances on them.)*
>
> IF YOU'RE GONNA MAKE ME TAKE YOUR BULL
> I'M GONNA TAKE IT BY THE HORNS
> AIN'T GONNA BE NO PUNCHES THAT I PULL
> WHEN I'M STOMPIN' ON YOUR CORNS!

SCALAWAG.
> GIRL, YOU'RE MAKING ME QUEASY!

SCUMBUCKET.
> SWEET LITTLE HONEY, TAKE IT EASY!

BELLA.
> AIN'T NO TIME TO FLIRT AND COO IT'S TIME TO PUT THE HURT ON YOU!
>
> *(She butts **SCALAWAG** and **SCUMBUCKET** so hard that they are flung out of the room. Far off gunshots are getting closer. **BELLA** scrambles over to **NATHANIEL**.)*

Mister Porter, we gotta get outta here.

NATHANIEL. Too late for me, little gal, I'm done for.

BELLA. Mister Porter, that's a flesh wound.

> (**NATHANIEL** *feels his chest, jumps up from the floor.*)

NATHANIEL. Why, so it is! But Bella, ain't no escape from this trap – only way out's the window, and we're too high up on the trestle to jump.

BELLA.
MISTER PORTER, I GOT ME AN IDEA!
NOW, WONCHA COME OVER HERE
AND LET ME WHISPER IN YOUR EAR!

> (*She whispers her idea into* **NATHANIEL**'s *ear.*)

(WHISPER, WHISPER, WHISPER, WHISPER
WHISPER, WHISPER, WHISPER...)

NATHANIEL.
SAY WHAT?!

BELLA.
(WHISPER, WHISPER, WHISPER, WHISPER
WHISPER, WHISPER, WHISPER...)

NATHANIEL. Wait a minute, wait a minute, wait a minute. Let me get this straight –
YOU SAY I JUMP ON YOUR LAP?

BELLA.
MM HM

NATHANIEL.
AND THEN WE SPRING FROM THIS TRAP?

BELLA.
MM HM

NATHANIEL.
AND THEN YOU LAND ON YOUR BEHIND?

BELLA.
THAT'S RIGHT

NATHANIEL.
YOU MUST BE OUT OF YOUR MIND, MIND, MIND!

SCOOTAH. (*Offstage.*) Snaggletooth. Skeetah, Scalawag, Scumbucket. I say, where the devil are you chaps?

(**BELLA** *climbs out the window.*)

BELLA. We ain't got time to debate my sanity. Now listen here...

YOU MUST FACE, MY SAVIN' GRACE

(*Patting her behind.*)

IS THIS HERE SECRET WEAPON!
MISTER PORTER, TRUST IN ME
AND LET US GET TO STEPPIN'!

(**NATHANIEL** *climbs out of the window.* **SNAGGLETOOTH** *awakens and blinks in disbelief as he watches* **NATHANIEL** *climb onto* **BELLA**'s *lap.*)

SNAGGLETOOTH. What the Sam Hill –
EYES ROLLIN' OUT OF MY SOCKETS
THE MAN DONE CLIMBED HER HIGH POCKETS
WITHOUT NO FURTHER PEEP

(*As they jump.*)

DONE TOOK A FLYIN' LEAP!

(*Running over to the window.*)

Well, I'll be ding-dang-dong-di-danged-di-dang-danged!

(*As* **BELLA** *and* **NATHANIEL** *"bounce" in and out of view through the window.*)

NATHANIEL.
AAAHHHH!
BELLA
AND NOW WE'RE FREE
NATHANIEL.
AAAHHHH!
BELLA & NATHANIEL.
AND WE WILL BE A-BOUNCIN' BACK 'TIL ETERNITY

Scene Fifteen

(**BELLA** *and* **NATHANIEL** *bounce down a mountainside. Birds and wild* **ANIMALS** *can be seen scrambling out of their path of descent.*)

BELLA. *(Giggling.)* Did you see the look on that ol' outlaw's face? Bet he'll think twice before he rob a train again.

(**NATHANIEL** *moans with terror.*)

NATHANIEL. He ain't the only one who shoulda thought twice.

BELLA. Mister Porter, you sound concerned.

[MUSIC NO. 13 "ROLLIN' ALONG"]

NATHANIEL. You ain't concerned that what we're doin' is impossible?

BELLA. How could it be impossible? We doin' it.

NATHANIEL. And we hittin' ev'ry last rock and ledge and – ow! – tree branch in the process. We shoulda taken our chances in the train – sure couldn't be any worse than what we're going through right now.

BELLA. You know somethin', Mister Porter?
SOME PEOPLE WOULD LIKE FOR THEIR LIVES TO BE
ALL WRAPPED UP IN WOOL

NATHANIEL. Wrapped up in wool would be great right about now.

BELLA.
SO MAD THAT THE GLASS IS HALF-EMPTY
THEY CAN'T SEE IT'S HALF-FULL

NATHANIEL. This glass is way more than half-empty.

BELLA.
SO THEY SNEER WITH THEIR LIP ALL CURLED
DON'T WANNA LISTEN
A BRAND NEW WAY TO LOOK AT THE WORLD
THAT'S WHAT THEY MISSIN'!

NATHANIEL.
>AND SOME PEOPLE LIKE TO TALK A LOTTA STUFF
>FROM OUT THE BACK OF A BULL

BELLA.
>MAYBE SO, BUT ALL YOUR BELLY ACHIN'
>AIN'T GONNA STOP US FROM ROLLIN' ALONG
>AIN'T GONNA STOP US FROM ROLLIN' ALONG
>AIN'T GONNA STOP US FROM ROLLIN' ALONG
>IN OL' GRAVITY'S PULL

NATHANIEL. I'm aware of gravity's pull, Bella – that's the problem!

BELLA. Ooh, look at that cliff wall, Mister Porter – I think I'ma ricochet off it.

NATHANIEL. You're gonna what?

BELLA. Yeah, it's gonna get us down faster.

NATHANIEL. I don't wanna go down faster, this is fast enough!

BELLA. Come on, it'll be fun!

NATHANIEL. Plummeting to certain death ain't fun!

*(With a chiding sigh, as some friendly turtledoves fly alongside **BELLA** to lend support.)*

BELLA. Mister Porter.

BELLA.	**TURTLEDOVES.**
SOME PEOPLE COMPLAIN THAT LIFE AIN'T NOTHIN' BUT A	COOOO WOOOO WOOOO

BELLA & TURTLEDOVES.
>BUMPY ROAD

NATHANIEL.
>OH LORD, THIS CAN'T BE HAPP'NIN'!

BELLA.	**TURTLEDOVES.**
THEY LIKE TO MOAN AND GROAN WHEN THEY CARRYIN' A	COOOO WOOOO WOOOO

BELLA & TURTLEDOVES.
HEAVY LOAD!

> (**NATHANIEL** *shrieks, as* **BELLA** *obliviously bounces towards a grizzly bear.*)

NATHANIEL.
BEAR! BEAR! BEAR! BEAR, BEAR, BEAR, BEAR, TO THE LEFT!

> (*Changing course,* **BELLA** *reaches out to pet a nearby cat on a ledge.*)

BELLA.
BUT THERE AIN'T NO SENSE IN CRYIN', RIGHT KITTY?

NATHANIEL.
BELLA, THAT'S A MOUNTAIN LION!

> (**BELLA** *pulls back her hand before the beast can rip it off.*)

BELLA.
WELL THAT'S A PITY, BUT A

BELLA.	**TURTLEDOVES.**
BEAR OR A MOUNTAIN LION OR A	COOOO WOOOO WOOOO

BELLA & TURTLEDOVES.
WARTY OL' TOAD!

WARTY OL' TOAD. (*Ogling* **BELLA.**)
RIBBIT! RIBBIT! RIBBIT! RIBBIT! YOW!

BELLA.
AIN'T GONNA STOP US FROM ROLLIN' ALONG
AIN'T GONNA STOP US FROM ROLLIN' ALONG
AIN'T GONNA STOP US FROM ROLLIN' ALONG
IN LIFE'S WILD EPISODE

Okay hold on, we 'bout to ricochet.

> (*They bounce off the cliff wall. To* **NATHANIEL**'s *surprise, it's fun.*)

NATHANIEL. Hoo whee! That was even better than playin' Snail Away Rauley!

BELLA. I'ma let you in on a little secret.

IT AIN'T NOTHIN' BUT A DISTANT MEM'RY
I BELIEVE I WAS FIVE YEARS OLD
AT NIGHT I SAW SOMETHIN' SHIMM'RY
A LITTLE STAR THAT I WANTED TO HOLD
I CLIMBED UP TO THE TOP OF THE ROOF, 'CAUSE
THAT STAR I HAD TO REACH
MAMA CAME OUTSIDE, SAW ME UP THERE
OH MY LORD, SHE STARTED TO SCREECH
I GOT STARTLED, I SLIPPED
THEN WHAT HAPPENED BY ALL ACCOUNTS
I HIT THE GROUND, I SPRANG AND FLIPPED
HIGHER AND HIGHER AND HIGHER I BOUNCED
CURLED OVER WITH MY KNEES UP
BOUNCIN' ALL AROUND THE PLACE
I SWEAR I SAW THE MAN IN THE MOON
WITH A PUZZLED LOOK UPON HIS FACE

NATHANIEL. Did you ever get that star?

BELLA. Only thing I got that night was a whuppin'. But Mama just hit the top of the bed covers, and I pretended like it hurt.

NATHANIEL. Bella, you a caution.

(They laugh. Suddenly, BELLA stiffens.)

BELLA.	**NATHANIEL.**
OH NO OH NO	WHAT'S THE MATTER?

BELLA.
I'M GETTIN' A CHARLIE HORSE

NATHANIEL.
BELLA, AINT NO NEED TO PANIC
I'LL JUST MASSAGE YOUR LEG

BELLA.
WELL, YOU CAN MASSAGE MY LEG, BUT
THAT AIN'T QUITE WHERE IT IS

NATHANIEL.
WELL, IF THAT AIN'T WHERE IT IS, THEN...
...IF THAT AIN'T... WHERE IT... IS, THEN...

(Horrified realization.)

OH NO, OH NO

BELLA.
>MISTER PORTER

NATHANIEL.
>OH NO, OH NO

BELLA.
>CALM DOWN!
>THIS AIN'T NO TIME TO PANIC!

NATHANIEL.
>YES IT IS

BELLA.
>THIS AIN'T NO TIME TO PANIC!

NATHANIEL.
>WE'LL DIE, FALLIN' INTO A CHASM
>'CAUSE YOUR BOOTY GOT A MUSCLE SPASM

BELLA.
>MISTER PORTER, I SAY WE AIN'T!
>MISTER PORTER, DID... YOU JUST FAINT?
>
>*(Nervous giggle.)*
>
>SOME...

BELLA	TURTLEDOVES.
	COOOO WOOOO WOOOO
...PEOPLE WILL NOT LOSE THEIR COOL, ALTHOUGH THEY'RE FACIN' COLD FACTS	

TURTLEDOVES.
>TRY TO HEAD FOR THE GRASSY SLOPE

BELLA.	**TURTLEDOVES.**
LIKE, BONES COULD BE CRUSHED INTO POWDER IN SOME NECKS AND SOME BACKS	COOOO WOOOO WOOOO

TURTLEDOVES.
>OVER THERE NEAR THE ANTELOPE

BELLA.
>WHY DID I THINK THAT THIS
>METHOD OF TRAVEL COULD BE TRUSTED?
>I SHOULDA KNOWN MY
>BOUNCIN' MACHINE WOULD GET BUSTED!

TURTLEDOVES.

I'LL TRY TO FIX IT WITH SOME	COOOO WOOOO WOOOO
"SHAKE IT UP, WAKE IT UP" SMACKS!	

>*(As **BELLA** smacks one side of her behind.)*

TURTLEDOVES.
>ONE FOR FAITH AND...

>*(As she smacks the other side.)*

>ONE FOR HOPE

BELLA.
>DON'T WANNA STOP US FROM ROLLIN' ALONG
>DON'T WANNA STOP US FROM ROLLIN' ALONG
>DON'T WANNA STOP US FROM ROLLIN' ALONG
>COME ON BACKSIDE, RELAX!
>RELAX!

>*(As she and **NATHANIEL** hurtle towards the ground.)*

>RELAX! RELAX!

ACT II

Scene Sixteen

[MUSIC NO. 13A "ENTR'ACTE"]

[MUSIC NO. 14 "HEAVEN MUST BE TUPELO"]

(Early morning. Light filters through a forest of gum trees rising from a swamp pond. There are beautiful orchid-like flowers and Seminole pumpkin gourd plants growing nearby. **BELLA** *is lying down on the bank.)*

TOWNSPEOPLE. *(Angelically.)*
HEAVEN MUST BE TUPELO, HEAVEN MUST BE TUPELO
BACK TO TUPELO I'LL GO, CAN'T REMEMBER WHY I EVER
LEFT IT

*(***BELLA***, revived, stands up and brushes herself off. She sees a road sign.)*

BELLA. What do you know, I'm on the Natchez Trace!

(As she walks happily down the country road.)

SUNLIGHT A-POKIN' THROUGH THE MISTY DAWN
BUTTERFLY FLUTTERIN' BY
SOMEBODY COOKIN' SOME HOPPIN' JOHN
OR IS IT SWEET POTATO PIE?
EV'RYWHERE I LOOK IS SO FAMILIAR NOW
I KNOW IT LIKE THE BACK OF MY HAND
AIN'T ENOUGH WORDS TO TELL Y'ALL HOW
I LOVE MY MISSISSIPPI LAND, AND
HEAVEN MUST BE TUPELO, HEAVEN MUST BE TUPELO
BACK TO TUPELO I'LL GO, CAN'T REMEMBER WHY I EVER
LEFT IT

> *(She's entering the town of Tupelo. As she sees* **TOWNSPEOPLE** *she knows, she waves eagerly to them.)*

BELLA.
HI! HI! HI! HI, HI! HI, HI!
HI! HI!

> *(None of the* **TOWNSPEOPLE** *respond to her.)*

HEY!
HELLO?
HUH?

WHAT'S WRONG WITH ALL OF Y'ALL?
WHY AIN'T YA TALKIN' TO ME?
WHY ARE YA LOOKIN' THROUGH ME?

> *(Sulky, sucking her teeth.)*

HMPH!

SUNLIGHT POKIN' THROUGH THE MISTY DAWN
BUTTERFLY FLUTTERIN'...

> *(Annoyed, brushing it away.)*

– Get out my face.

PEOPLE ACTIN' FUNNY, SOMETHIN' STRANGE GOIN' ON
WHAT DO IT ALL SIGNIFY?

> *(She gasps.)*

Wait.

HERE COME A MEM'RY FLOWIN' THROUGH MY HEAD
DID I CRASH DOWN A MOUNTAINSIDE?

Yes, that's what I did.

YOU KNOW, I BETCHA I AM PROBABLY DEAD
IT'S A LIKELIHOOD THAT CANNOT BE DENIED
BUT IF I'M DEAD, AND I'M ON THE NATCHEZ TRACE
AND IF THE NATCHEZ TRACE AIN'T A HELLIFIED PLACE...
THEN...

TOWNSPEOPLE.	**BELLA.**
HEAVEN MUST BE TUPELO	I AM HOME

TOWNSPEOPLE.	BELLA.
HEAVEN MUST BE TUPELO	I AM HOME IN TUPELO
BACK TO TUPELO I'LL GO	
CAN'T REMEMBER WHY I	I AM HOME
EVER LEFT IT	
HEAVEN MUST BE TUPELO	AND IT'S AS BEAUTIFUL
HEAVEN MUST BE TUPELO	AS I REMEMBER
WHEN, TO TUPELO, I GO	ALL OF THE PEOPLE, AND
IT'LL BE JUST LIKE	ALL OF THE PLACES, AND
NEVER LEFT IT	ALL OF THE FEELINGS I
	LEFT BEHIND ME IN
HEAVEN MUST BE TUPELO	TUPELO
HEAVEN MUST BE TUPELO	TUPELO

ALL.
    I'VE COME HOME TO THE FINEST, DIVINEST PLACE I
        KNOW
    THE HEAVEN I CALL TUPELO!

Scene Seventeen

[MUSIC NO. 15 "INTRO TO BONNY JOHNNY RAKEHELL"]

(The town of Tupelo turns back into the swamp. **BONNY JOHNNY RAKEHELL,** *a wealthy southern gentleman steps into* **BELLA***'s path. He bears an astonishing resemblance to* **SNAGGLETOOTH HOSKINS,** *except he sports a dashing mustache.)*

BELLA. Oh no.

JOHNNY. *(Smirking.)* That's right.

IT'S BON...

BELLA.

– SNAGGLETOOTH HOSKINS!

JOHNNY.

WHO?

BELLA.

SNAGGLETOOTH!

JOHNNY. *(Offended.)*

SNAGGLETOOTH? SNAGGLETOOTH?
DO THESE LOOK LIKE SNAGGLETEETH TO YOU?

(A bell dings as he flashes a brilliant smile.)

[MUSIC NO. 15A "BONNY JOHNNY RAKEHELL"]

I'm

BONNY JOHNNY RAKEHELL
THE BEAU OF CHICKASAW
ALTHOUGH I COME FROM WAY DOWN SOUTH
I LIVE ABOVE THE LAW
SOME WOMEN CALL ME BONNY JOHN
SOME CALL ME LORD AND SAVIOR
BUT WHAT NO WOMAN EVER CALLS...
... IS ME, ON MY BEHAVIOR!

(Tupelo **TOWNSFOLK** *enter.)*

TOWNSFOLK.
>BONNY JOHNNY RAKEHELL

JOHNNY.
>I'M THE BANE OF ALL THE LADIES

TOWNSFOLK.
>BONNY JOHNNY RAKEHELL

JOHNNY
>I LOVE THE PAIN OF ALL THE LADIES
>IF YOU DON'T ESCAPE BEFORE
>I TAKE WHAT I WILL TAKE, WELL
>THAT'S THE WORST MISTAKE TO MAKE
>WITH BONNY JOHNNY RAKEHELL!

BELLA. Please, please, Mister, let me pass by.

JOHNNY. How can I let opportunity pass me by?

JOHNNY.	**TOWNSFOLK.**
YOU CAN'T DISTRACT A RAKEHELL	OOH!
FROM THE PLEASURE THAT HE SEEKS	OOH, OOH!
TO DALLY WITH A LOWLY MAID WILL	OOH, OOH!
GIVE HIM GOOD TECHNIQUES	OOH!
AND COLORED GAL, ADMIT IT	OOH!
YOU'RE THE LOWLIEST OF ALL	OOH, OOH!
STOP YOUR SILLY QUIBBLIN'	
AND DIVE INTO THE FALL, WITH	

TOWNSFOLK.
>BONNY JOHNNY RAKEHELL

JOHNNY
>I'M THE ONE WHO ALWAYS WINS

TOWNSFOLK
>BONNY JOHNNY RAKEHELL LOVES TO MAKE HELL

JOHNNY. *(Bowing with a flourish.)*
FOR MY SINS!
WHEN I HOLD YOU IN MY ARMS
SO TIGHTLY THAT YOU BREAK, WELL
MAYBE IT'S ASSAULT, BUT IT'S YOUR FAULT
SAYS JOHNNY RAKEHELL!

JOHNNY.	**BELLA & TOWNSFOLK.**
THE SOUND OF YOUR FEARS	NO, NO, NO, NO, NO, NO, NO, NO, NO!
IS MUSIC TO MY EARS	NO, NO, NO, NO, NO, NO, NO, NO, NO, NO, NO, NO!
THE SOUND OF YOUR HELL	NO, NO, NO, NO, NO, NO, NO, NO, NO!
IS ME	NO, NO, NO, NO!
LETTIN' OUT MY REBEL YELL!	

*(**JOHNNY** chases **BELLA**, doing his "rebel yell" war cry.)*

JOHNNY.	**TOWNSFOLK.**
AIEE-YAH	IF YOU TRY TO FIGHT BACK YOUR GRIEF WILL BE INTENSE
AIEE-YAH	'CAUSE JOHNNY AIN'T SO BONNY WHEN YOU PUT UP A DEFENSE

JOHNNY.
I'LL HAVE MY CAKE AND EAT IT TOO
AND IF YOU ARE MY CAKE, WELL
YOU MIGHT AS WELL ENJOY THE TRYST
IT'S, AFTER ALL, WHY YOU EXIST
NOW FACE THAT FACT OR FACE THE FIST
OF BONNY JOHNNY RAKEHELL! JOHNNY RAKEHELL!

Scene Eighteen

[MUSIC NO. 15B "BONNY JOHNNY RAKEHELL - REPRISE"]

(*As* BELLA *struggles with* JOHNNY.)

BELLA. Why you wanna hurt me, Mister? I ain't nothin' to you.

JOHNNY. You ain't nothin' to me, but I know who you are. You belong to the Patterson plantation.

BELLA. I don't belong to nobody. My daddy left that plantation to fight a war to make it so.

JOHNNY. Your daddy left the plantation in a pine box after he tried to stop Old Man Patterson from beddin' your big booty mama.

BELLA. My daddy fought in the war, I got a picture of him standin' right alongside President Abraham Lincoln on the battlefield.

JOHNNY. I don't know who's standin' beside that nigger lover but ain't your daddy, 'cause Old Man Patterson shot that rascal 'fore he could set foot off the plantation.

BELLA. It ain't true, let me go, I'll tell on you, Mister, I will.

JOHNNY. And who's gonna believe your tragic tale?

VOICE OF SPIRIT OF THE BOOTY. I will.

BELLA. Who said that?

[MUSIC NO. 16 "ONE ASS TO ANOTHER - INTRO"]

VOICE OF SPIRIT OF THE BOOTY. It is I, your ancestor, the Itty Bitty Gal. On a ship of misery, from far across the sea I have come here to tell you that that man is talking out of his ass. And now it is time for you to talk out of yours.

Scene Nineteen

[MUSIC NO. 16A "ONE ASS TO ANOTHER"]

(Bubbling, gurgling swamp river noise.)

VOICE OF SPIRIT OF THE BOOTY.
OOOH... OOOH... OOOH...

JOHNNY.
WHAT IS THAT SOUND, MURM'RING SOFT AND LOW?

VOICE OF SPIRIT OF THE BOOTY.
IT'S BELLA'S ASS, AND IT'S ABOUT TO SHOW

(Orchid-like flowers and gourd plants animate and begin to resemble female body parts. Out of the swamp rises a woman. As she continues to rise out of the water, the lower part of her anatomy contains the largest, most mythically proportioned, the most gloriously shaped black woman's booty in existence. The woman – **SPIRIT OF THE BOOTY** *– steps onto the land and switches over to* **JOHNNY.***)*

JOHNNY. Noooo.

SPIRIT OF THE BOOTY. Yaasssssss.

JOHNNY.	**SWAMP PLANTS.**
Stay away. You ain't talkin' to me, you ain't talkin' to me.	

SPIRIT OF THE BOOTY.

If only you'd realized that about all them other female body parts you thought was talkin' to you. But since you didn't,	OOH, OOH OOH, OOH OOH, OOH
FOR THE PAIN AND THE SUFFERIN'	
YOU BEEN PUTTIN' WOMEN THROUGH	OOH

SPIRIT OF THE BOOTY.	**SWAMP PLANTS.**
I AM HERE TO KNOCK THE EVERLOVIN'	
DAYLIGHTS OUT OF YOU	OOH
PAYBACK TIME, THE JIG IS UP, BROTHER	OOH
NOW YOU AND ME 'BOUT TO DEAL WITH IT	OOH
ONE ASS TO ANOTHER,	OOH
ONE ASS TO ANOTHER	OOH
NOW YOU AND ME 'BOUT TO DEAL WITH IT	OOH
ONE ASS TO ANOTHER,	OOH
YEAH	OOH

BELLA.

> NO
> AIN'T NO NEED FOR ALTERCATION
> BOOTY, HEAR ME WHEN I SPEAK
> VIOLENCE CAN'T BE THE ANSWER
> BOOTY, TURN THE OTHER CHEEK

SPIRIT OF THE BOOTY.

> GIRL, IF YOU DON'T WANT TO SEE THIS
> THEN YOUR EYES YOU BETTER CLOSE
> AND IF YOU DON'T WANT TO SMELL IT
> GIRL, YOU BETTER HOLD YOUR NOSE

> *(All the rage of **BELLA**'s brutalized and raped female ancestors concentrates itself into **BELLA**'s magical behind. She's getting a squirmy feeling in her intestines.)*

SPIRIT OF THE BOOTY & SWAMP PLANTS.

> IT'S TIME TO ATTACK FROM BEHIND
> THIS TACKY ATTACKER OF WOMANKIND
> LET YOUR GUT FEELINGS AND YOUR DESPERATION
> GIVE IN TO A FUNKY SENSATION

BELLA.

> I CAN'T STOP THIS FEELIN' I GOT

SPIRIT OF THE BOOTY & SWAMP PLANTS.

> LET IT GO

BELLA.
>THE KIND OF FEELIN' WHERE YOU NEED A CHAMBER POT

SPIRIT OF THE BOOTY & SWAMP PLANTS.
>LET IT GO

BELLA. *(Panicking.)*
>I CAN'T HOLD IT IN, IT'S EV'RYWHERE

>>*(The fury from her bowels is unleashed, with a stench as rotten as oppression.)*

SPIRIT OF THE BOOTY & SWAMP PLANTS.
>LET IT SPLATTER ON HIS CLOTHES
>ON HIS FACE AND IN HIS HAIR
>'CAUSE WHEN HE

SPIRIT OF THE BOOTY.	**SWAMP PLANTS.**
TRIED TO TAKE YOUR VIRTUE	OOH
HE PROMPTED MY AGGRESSION	OOH
I GOT TOO MUCH BOTTOM TO BOW TO HIS OPPRESSION	OOH
I'M GONNA MAKE HIM CRY FOR HIS MOTHER	OOH
NOTHIN' CAN STOP ME DEALIN' WITH HIM	OOH

SPIRIT OF THE BOOTY.
>ONE ASS TO ANOTHER

>>*(As they do a nineteenth century "swamp twerk" with each other.)*

SWAMP PLANTS.
>ONE ASS TO ANOTHER

SPIRIT OF THE BOOTY.
>ONE ASS TO ANOTHER
>IT'S THE PERFECT TIME AND PLACE
>TO BE DEALIN' FACE TO FACE
>ONE ASS TO ANOTHER

SWAMP PLANTS.
> ONE ASS TO ANOTHER

SPIRIT OF THE BOOTY.
> ONE ASS TO ANOTHER

SWAMP PLANTS.
> ONE ASS TO ANOTHER

SPIRIT OF THE BOOTY.
> ONE ASS TO ANOTHER

SWAMP PLANTS.
> ONE ASS TO ANOTHER

> *(With a magical gesture the **SPIRIT OF THE BOOTY** puts **BELLA** to sleep and drags a flailing screaming **JOHNNY** into the depths of the swamp.)*

SPIRIT OF THE BOOTY.
> ONE ASS TO ANOTHER

Scene Twenty

(A big top circus tent has formed around **BELLA** *as she tosses and turns in her sleep.)*

BELLA. ... It was an accident...Itty Bitty Gal, don't leave me...oh Mama...oh Grandma...oh Mister Porter, watch out for the bird's nest...

(She jolts up. The owner of the circus, **CP CONYERS**, *and his disfigured and deformed brother,* **GABRIEL** *are now standing over her.)*

The train – where's Mister Porter?

CONYERS. Colored man who fell through the roof with you? He's dead. It's a miracle you survived.

BELLA. Mister Porter...dead?

(She breaks down weeping.)

We was high up on a trestle and I thought my backside had enough spring in it to cushion the fall, so we jumped out the window. We was bouncin' down the side of the mountain.

We almost made it, but the springiness back there done give out at the last minute, oh, poor Mister Porter.

CONYERS. What's your name, gal?

BELLA. Bella Patter – Bella Johnson.

CONYERS. Yeah, Bella, that's what your friend called you before he kicked the bucket.

*(***BELLA*** starts wailing.)*

GABRIEL. Why are you lying about that man dying, CP?

*(***CONYERS*** grabs ***GABRIEL***.)*

CONYERS. Because, you idiot – I gotta have her in the circus.

GABRIEL. *(Wincing in pain.)* CP, you're br-breaking m-my arm –

BELLA. You stop hurtin' him.

CONYERS. Sorry. Did you hear that, freak? For some ungodly reason she seems to like you. Well, I've gotta go talk the Two-Headed Nightingale out of quitting again. This is your chance to do something for me, for once in your life, Gabriel. Don't let me down.

(Pushing **GABRIEL** *to* **BELLA.** *He exits.)*

BELLA. I don't like him.

GABRIEL. He's not so bad once you get to know him.

BELLA. *(Crying.)* I don't want to get to know him. I want to go home.

GABRIEL. Now, Miss Johnson, don't get yourself upset. Mister Porter wouldn't want that. Why, right at the end he said, "Tell Bella not to fret, I'm going to a better place."

BELLA. He did?

GABRIEL. He said the happiest moments of his life were bouncing down that mountain with you.

*(***BELLA** *impulsively clasps his hand.)*

BELLA. Oh, thank you.

[MUSIC NO. 17 "BIDE A LITTLE TIME AT THE CIRCUS"]

GABRIEL. What are you going to do now?

BELLA. Ain't got the slightest idea. I ain't got no money now – I left it on the train.

Scene Twenty-One

GABRIEL. I know how you can make a little money.
BELLA. How?

> *(The scene becomes a circus show.* **GABRIEL** *guides her through it.)*

GABRIEL.
BIDE A LITTLE T-TIME AT THE C-CIRCUS
BELLA. At the circus?
GABRIEL.
SEIZE AN OPPORTUNITY R-RARE
WATCH GR-GRACEFUL BALLERINAS
PLAY GOLDEN CONCER-T-T-TINAS
AS ACROBATS FL-FLY THROUGH THE A-A-AIR
BELLA. Will you look at that!
GABRIEL.
NOW, WHEN YOU'VE SEEN THE M-MAN-EATING L-LION
BELLA. Y'all got a lion?
GABRIEL.
YOU'LL HAVE TR-TROUBLE SLEEPING FOR WEEKS
BELLA. Oh my.
GABRIEL.
AND ONCE INSIDE THE TENT, YOU
WILL SCREAM –

> *(***BELLA*** shrieks and laughs as he playfully jumps at her.)*

BELLA. Aaahh!
GABRIEL.
– WHEN WE PRESENT YOU
WITH OUTLANDISH, ABNORMAL FREAKS!
BELLA.
I WAS NOT THE BEST PUPIL, MY TEACHERS WOULD SAY
NEVER PICKED FOR THE TEAM
WHEN MY SCHOOLMATES WOULD PLAY
BUT I HAD ME THIS BOOK THAT COULD TAKE ME AWAY
IT WAS ALL ABOUT TRAV'LIN' THE WORLD

GABRIEL. Travel the world with us, and make money while you're doing it.

BELLA. How much money?

GABRIEL. A hundred dollars.

BELLA. A hundred dollars – that's more money than I can even imagine! But I can't be stayin' with the circus for no year, I got to get to my sweetheart.

GABRIEL. No, Miss J-Johnson –

BELLA. Call me Bella.

GABRIEL. Not a year, B-Bella. A week.

BELLA. A hundred dollars a week – you so funny... You ain't jokin'?

GABRIEL. *(Offering his hand.)* No joke. What do you say?

BELLA. *(Shaking GABRIEL's hand.)*
  YES

BELLA & GABRIEL.
  BIDE A LITTLE TIME
  AT THE CIRCUS
  SEIZE AN OPPORTUNITY RARE
  WATCH GRACEFUL BALLERINAS
  PLAY GOLDEN CONCERTINAS
  AS ACROBATS
  FLY THROUGH THE AIR!
  WHEN YOU'VE SEEN THE
  MAN-EATING LION
  YOU'LL HAVE TROUBLE SLEEPING FOR WEEKS
  AND ONCE INSIDE
  THE TENT, YOU
  WILL SCREAM WHEN WE PRESENT YOU
  WITH OUTLANDISH
  ABNORMAL FREAKS!

GABRIEL.
  BIDE A LITTLE TIME AT THE CIRCUS
  TIME TO TRAVEL THE WORLD

Scene Twenty-Two

(Nearby the circus, **NATHANIEL** *lies unconscious. A farmer and his wife,* **MR.** *and* **MRS. DINWIDDIE** *are heading home from the circus.)*

MRS. DINWIDDIE. Wasn't that a wonderful show, Mr. Dinwiddie?

MR. DINWIDDIE. Worth every penny we done spent, Mrs. Dinwiddie. I can't decide which act was my favorite, they was all so spectacular.

MRS. DINWIDDIE. How 'bout when the four-legged tap dancer did the splits?

MR. DINWIDDIE. Ooh the turp-see-corey-inn splendor, and then, when that armless-legless man did them cartwheels, I didn't think he was never gonna stop.

MRS. DINWIDDIE. I swanee, I was all on tenterhooks.

(Grabbing **MR. DINWIDDIE***'s arm in excited remembrance.)*

The Paw-Dee-Doo between the Strong Man and the elephant –

MR. DINWIDDIE. The Waltz of The Peanut – when he Pee-Row-Wetted up and down his trunk –

MRS. DINWIDDIE. Ooh, I like to weep pure tears of joy.

MR. DINWIDDIE. That wasn't even the extravaganza in the big tent –

MRS. DINWIDDIE. We just gotta come back tomorrow before they leave our town, Mr. Dinwiddie. We won't get another chance until next year.

MR. DINWIDDIE. How we gonna do that and we done used up our savin's?

MRS. DINWIDDIE. Can't we mortgage the lower back forty?

MR. DINWIDDIE. I s'pose we could do that, I s'pose – whoa, whoa, whoa, what's this over here?

MRS. DINWIDDIE. Why, it looks to be an unconscious Pullman Porter.

MR. DINWIDDIE. Whatcha s'pose happened to him?

MRS. DINWIDDIE. Well, judgin' from this flesh wound, and this mud here from a cliff bird's nest and these scraps of tattered canvas strewn all over him, only one thing coulda happened. This man was wounded by a train robber, and had to escape by jumpin' off the side of a mountain, then he fell through the roof of a circus tent.

MR. DINWIDDIE. Your sloothin' skills never fail to impress.

MRS. DINWIDDIE. I only calls it as I sees it. And judgin' by the fact that he been drug over here and left for dead, somebody in that circus must not have wanted him around. What he needs is help.

MR. DINWIDDIE. The help of two good sum-marry-tins like us.

MRS. DINWIDDIE. Like us, Mr. Dinwiddie. 'Cause it's a wicked, wicked world we live in.

MR. DINWIDDIE. Just so, Mrs. Dinwiddie, just so.

(They exit.)

Scene Twenty-Three

[MUSIC NO. 17A "TUNING"]

*(At the circus, **GABRIEL** is rehearsing a jungle scene. He reads.)*

GABRIEL. And now, l-ladies and gentlemen, boys and girls, the moment you've all been waiting for.

*(Calling to **BELLA**, who's behind a curtain.)*

Bella, the script says you've got to be standing over there on your m-mark.

*(**BELLA** comes through the curtain. She's wearing a skimpy, unattractive, and offensive "jungle" costume. **GABRIEL** stares, appalled.)*

Dear God. I didn't come up with that costume, I swear to you.

*(**CONYERS** enters in full whiteface, wearing a safari outfit complete with rifle and pith helmet.)*

CONYERS. Isn't it perfect? Nothing says Africa like a half naked woman with a big booty. The crowds are gonna eat you up, gal – ooh, almost forgot. I made a few extra changes to the script.

GABRIEL. *(Reading the new script.)* Princess Unga Bunga?

CONYERS. Doesn't it have a ring to it? Well, only thirty minutes to showtime, keep rehearsing.

(He exits.)

BELLA. I ain't gonna do it, Gabriel, I ain't.

GABRIEL. Hold on a second.

(He takes out a pen, starts crossing out lines on the script and replacing them with new ones.)

What if –

*(**BELLA** reads what he's written.)*

BELLA. And then put this in, too?

(She writes something.)

GABRIEL. In for a penny...

BELLA. In for a pound.

[MUSIC NO. 18 "WHITE PEOPLE TONIGHT"]

*(They exit, continuing to edit the script as they giggle. Spotlight up on **CONYERS** standing in front of the jungle scene. Drumbeats.)*

Scene Twenty-Four

CONYERS. Ladies and gentlemen, boys and girls, welcome to the CP Conyers Traveling Circus.

> *(He gestures for applause. As they applaud.)*

Now it is time to present to you a phenomenon so incredible, you simply will not believe your eyes. Straight from deepest, darkest Africa, I bring you the deepest darkest tale you'll ever hear. The tale of Princess Unga Bunga.

> *(**BELLA** enters in her costume.)*

The princess was the ruler of a savage, primitive tribe. One day, an intrepid explorer –

> *(Indicating himself.)*

– Happened upon her village at dinner time. He raised his hand in greeting and cried out, "Unga Bunga! Bunga Unga!" Which means: Bow down to the Great White Father, jungle princess. It is time you learned to recognize your natural master –

> *(He is distracted by the entrance of a loincloth clad **GABRIEL**. Puzzled, he watches as **GABRIEL** pushes a giant cooking pot on wheels to the center of the stage, then exits on the other side.)*

– Time you learned to recognize your natural master. For it is the God-given destiny of the inferior races of the world to serve white people. The princess called forth her people to deliver the news.

> *(Hand cupped to mouth like Glinda in* The Wizard of Oz, **BELLA** *sweetly calls out.)*

BELLA.
  IT'S UNGA BUNGA TIME TO SERVE THE NIGHT MEAL

> *(Like slack-jawed, dull-witted Munchkins, the **VILLAGERS** enter.)*

VILLAGERS.
UNGA BUNGA, UNGA BUNGA, UNGA BUNGA, BUNGA!
BELLA.
WE UNGA BUNGANS LOVE TO EAT THE RIGHT MEAL
VILLAGERS.
UNGA BUNGA, UNGA BUNGA, UNGA BUNGA, BUNGA!
BELLA.
AND SINCE WE KNOW IT'S BEST TO EAT A LIGHT MEAL
VILLAGERS.
UNGA BUNGA, UNGA BUNGA, UNGA BUNGA, BUNGA!
BELLA.
TONIGHT WILL BE OUR LIGHTEST MEAL OF ALL

(In an unexpected move, the **VILLAGERS** *grab* **CONYERS**, *lift him on their shoulders and march him around the village, chanting.)*

VILLAGERS.	**CONYERS.**
UNGA BUNGA, UNGA BUNGA, UNGA BUNGA, UNGA BUNGA!	Wait a minute! What the hell's going on? This isn't in the script!
UNGA BUNGA, UNGA BUNGA, UNGA BUNGA, UNGA BUNGA	Put me down! This is your Great White Father speaking! Put me down!

(The **VILLAGERS** *dump him into the pot.)*

MALE VILLAGERS.	**FEMALE VILLAGERS.**	**CONYERS.**
UNGA BUNGA, UNGA BUNGA	UNGA BUNGA	What the hell do you think you're doing?
UNGA BUNGA, UNGA BUNGA	UNGA BUNGA	
UNGA BUNGA UNGA BUNGA UNGA BUNGA UNG!	UNGA BUNGA UNG!	

(**BELLA** *rips off her raggedy jungle costume to reveal a fabulous Josephine Baker outfit.*)

BELLA.
>WE SERVIN'
>WHITE PEOPLE TONIGHT
>WHITE PEOPLE TONIGHT
>CRUNCHY, MUNCHY, JUICY, TASTY
>WHITE PEOPLE TONIGHT
>
>WHITE PEOPLE TONIGHT
>WHITE PEOPLE TONIGHT
>THEY A LITTLE UNDONE
>BUT WITH A HOT CROSS BUN
>WE GONNA SEASON THEM UP JUST RIGHT

(**BELLA** *does an interpretive dance around the pot.*)

GABRIEL & MALE VILLAGERS.	**FEMALE VILLAGERS.**
WHAT'S COOKIN',	PRINCESS UNGA BUNGA?
WHAT'S COOKIN',	PRINCESS UNGA BUNGA?
WHAT'S COOKIN',	PRINCESS UNGA BUNGA?

GABRIEL & VILLAGERS.
>SMELLS SO GOOD, MY TASTEBUDS ACHE!

GABRIEL & MALE VILLAGERS.	**FEMALE VILLAGERS.**
WHAT'S COOKIN',	PRINCESS UNGA BUNGA?
WHAT'S COOKIN',	PRINCESS UNGA BUNGA?
WHAT'S COOKIN',	PRINCESS UNGA BUNGA?

BELLA.
>RED EYE GRAVY AND CHICKEN FRIED FAKE

(*To* **CONYERS** *in the pot.*)

>GREAT WHITE FATHER, DON'T LET ME UNNERVE YOU
>BUT COOKIN' YOU'S THE ONLY WAY I'M EVER GONNA SERVE YOU

GABRIEL & VILLAGERS.
>UNGA BUNGA! SERVES YOU RIGHT

BELLA.
>WHITE PEOPLE TONIGHT

GABRIEL & VILLAGERS.
>YUM, YUM YUM!

BELLA.
>WHITE PEOPLE TONIGHT

GABRIEL & VILLAGERS.
>YUM, YUM!

BELLA.
>CRUNCHY, MUNCHY, CHEESEY, CORNY
>WHITE PEOPLE TONIGHT
>I THINK I'D BETTER STIR THE POT

GABRIEL & VILLAGERS.
>WELL, IF YOU THINK YOU OUGHTA

BELLA.
>I THINK THAT SUPPER'S GETTIN' HOT

GABRIEL & VILLAGERS.
>MMMMMMMMMM! MAKES MY MOUTH WATER!

>>(**CONYERS,** *noticing the audience's enjoyment, gets into the swing of things.*)

>WHITE PEOPLE TONIGHT

BELLA & CONYERS.
>YOU BET IT!

GABRIEL & VILLAGERS.
>WHITE PEOPLE TONIGHT

BELLA & CONYERS.
>COME AND GET IT!

GABRIEL & VILLAGERS.
>CRUNCHY, MUNCHY, JUICY, TASTY
>WHITE PEOPLE TONIGHT

BELLA.
>THEY A LITTLE UNDONE

CONYERS.
>BUT WITH A HOT CROSS BUN

BELLA & CONYERS.
>YOU'RE GONNA WANNA TAKE A BITE

BELLA.
>OF CRUNCHY

CONYERS.
    MUNCHY
BELLA.
    JUICY
CONYERS.
    TASTY
BELLA.
    STEAMY
CONYERS.
    CREAMY
BELLA.
    PINK
CONYERS.
    AND PASTY
BELLA.
    WHITE
CONYERS.
    WHITE
BELLA.
    WHITE
CONYERS.
    WHITE
BELLA.
    WHITE
CONYERS.
    WHITE
BELLA.
    WHITE
CONYERS.
    WHITE
BELLA, CONYERS, GABRIEL & VILLAGERS.
    WHITE, WHITE, WHITE, WHITE, WHITE
BELLA.
    WHITE PEOPLE TONIGHT!
CONYERS, GABRIEL & VILLAGERS.
    WHITE PEOPLE TONIGHT!

BELLA.
>WHITE PEOPLE TONIGHT!

CONYERS, GABRIEL & VILLAGERS.
>WHITE PEOPLE TONIGHT!

BELLA.
>WHITE PEOPLE TONIGHT!

CONYERS, GABRIEL & VILLAGERS.
>WHITE PEOPLE TONIGHT!

ALL.
>WHITE PEOPLE TONIGHT!
>*(SLURP!)*

Scene Twenty-Five

[MUSIC NO. 18A "WHITE PEOPLE TONIGHT - UNDERSCORE"]

(BELLA, GABRIEL, *and* CONYERS *stand as if behind a curtain, as the audience wildly applauds on the other side of it.*)

AUDIENCE MEMBER 1. More, more!

CONYERS. You hear that? What a show.

AUDIENCE MEMBER 2. Bring the big booty gal back!

BELLA. They talkin' 'bout me.

AUDIENCE MEMBER 3. I'm comin' tomorrow night to see that big booty gal and I'm bringin' my whole family!

AUDIENCE MEMBERS. Big Booty! Big Booty! Big Booty! Big Booty!

(*As the audience continues chanting.*)

CONYERS. (*To* **BELLA**.) You're sitting on a gold mine, gal. Tickets are gonna sell like hotcakes.

BELLA. That star I been tryin' to reach for – it's me.

CONYERS. That's right Bella, and you need to shine in bright new places, places like London, Paris, Madrid, Berlin.

BELLA. Trav'lin' the world.

GABRIEL. Wait a minute, what about New M-Mexico?

BELLA. What about New Mexico?

GABRIEL. Your betrothed.

BELLA. Oh yeah, Aloysius – he can wait, I'm Bella Patterson, I'm a star and on the world stage is where I belong.

(*She makes a grand exit, stumbling because her nose is too high in the air to see where she's going.*)

GABRIEL. Patterson – I thought she said her name was J-Johnson.

CONYERS. Who cares about her name, it's her booty that's important.

Scene Twenty-Six

(**MAMA**, **GRANDMA**, *and* **AUNT DINAH** *are at home.* **GRANDMA** *looks at a poster of* **BELLA**. **AUNT DINAH** *is counting a pile of money.*)

GRANDMA. Read it to me again.

MAMA. I done read it to you ten times already, Mama.

AUNT DINAH. But why ain't you happy, Sister? Look at all this money Bella sendin' us, now she a big star, she trav'lin' all around the world.

MAMA. Either you done forgot how to read or your mind goin' the same way as Mama's, look at the poster, Sister.

[MUSIC NO. 18B "WELL, SLAP MY KNEE"]

AUNT DINAH. It say Bella Patterson, the Big Booty Tupelo – *(Gasp!)* it say Bella *Patterson*.

MAMA. She done put her real name on the poster, I'm so worried Bonny Johnny gonna find out –

GRANDMA. You ain't got to worry 'bout that, he already know –

(**MAMA** *grabs* **GRANDMA**, *who is halfway out of the door.*)

MAMA. Mama, where you think you goin'?

GRANDMA. Who y'all?

MAMA. Your daughters, Mama.

GRANDMA. Oh yeah. Well, me and Itty Bitty Gal goin' to see Bella.

MAMA. You ain't goin' nowhere, stop tryin' to run away.

GRANDMA. But I got to warn her –

MAMA. Let Itty Bitty Gal do that, you come back in this house.

GRANDMA. But Bonny Johnny lookin' at the poster right now, and he goin' –

(*As* **BONNY JOHNNY** *appears on another part of the stage, reading the poster.*)

JOHNNY.
>WELL, SLAP MY KNEE AND MAKE ME A PEANUT BUTTER SANDWICH
>'CAUSE LOOKS LIKE SOMEBODY'S PAST
>SOMEBODY'S DEEP DARK BIG BOOTY PAST
>IS 'BOUT TO CATCH UP WITH HER –
>Ha ha ha
>NOW AIN'T THAT GOOD NEWS? MM HMM

>>*(CONYERS in a spotlight.)*

>>## [MUSIC NO. 19 "TRAV'LIN' THE WORLD"]

CONYERS. And now, ladies and gentlemen, CP Conyers proudly presents that world famous international star, Bella Patterson, the Big Booty Tupelo Gal.

>>*(BELLA struts onstage to applause and cheers. She wears a snazzy costume. CONYERS and GABRIEL join her: they're her backup boy dancers.)*

BELLA.
>I WAS NOT THE BEST PUPIL, MY TEACHERS WOULD SAY

>>*(CONYERS and GABRIEL are Englishmen, with upper crust accents.)*

CONYERS & GABRIEL.
>SHE IS A SWEETIE AND A HONEY AND A CUTIE

BELLA.
>NEVER PICKED FOR THE TEAM WHEN MY SCHOOLMATES WOULD PLAY

CONYERS & GABRIEL.
>SHE IS A LADY WITH A MAHVELOUS PATOOTIE

BELLA.
>BUT I HAD ME THIS BOOK THAT COULD TAKE ME AWAY

CONYERS & GABRIEL.
>WHAT WAS THE SUBJECT?

BELLA.
>IT WAS ALL ABOUT TRAV'LIN THE WORLD

CONYERS & GABRIEL.
>HER GLORIOUS MUSCLE IS CAUSING A RUSTLE
>>*(They turn around, they're wearing protruding bustles.)*
>
>THAT GIRL IS THE REASON FOR THE INVENTION OF THE BUSTLE

BELLA.
>IT HAD PICTURES OF FOLKS AT THEM LONDON TOWN BALLS

CONYERS.
>JOLLY GOOD!

GABRIEL.
>SPOT ON!

CONYERS.
>I SAY!

GABRIEL.
>PIP, PIP!

CONYERS.
>CHEERIO

GABRIEL.
>AND ALL THAT ROT!

BELLA.
>IT HAD COWBOYS WHO'D DUKE IT OUT IN SALOON HALLS
>>*(**CONYERS** and **GABRIEL** are now **COWBOYS** in a barroom brawl.)*

CONYERS.
>SHUT YER YAP!

GABRIEL.
>SHUT YER GOB!

CONYERS & GABRIEL.
>MAKE YER MOVE! SHOOT YER SHOT!

BELLA.
>FROM THE BANKS OF THE NILE TO VICTORIA FALLS
>>*(**CONYERS** and **GABRIEL** are now explorers, a javelin lands near them.)*

CONYERS & GABRIEL.
>BEWARE THE JAV'LIN!

BELLA.
>I LEARNED ALL ABOUT TRAV'LIN' THE WORLD

>>(**CONYERS** *and* **GABRIEL** *are now Frenchmen.*)

CONYERS & GABRIEL.
>NOW ZAT POOR LEETLE BOOKWORM FROM TUPELO'S
>BECOME A REECH SOPHISTICATED CINDERELLA
>SHE'S SWEEPING THROUGH ZE LAND BY POPULAR DEMAND

CONYERS, GABRIEL & CIRCUS FOLKS.
>EV'RYBODY WANTS TO SEE BELLA!

>>(**CONYERS** *and* **GABRIEL** *are now Germans.*)

CONYERS & GABRIEL.
>SHE IST BOOKING AMPHITHEATERS, VIS RECORD CROWDS IN EVERY CITY!
>EVERY COUNTRY!
>EV'RY NATION
>IF YOU'D LIKE TO GAZE UPON DIS TRUE PHENOMENON
>VE SUGGEST YOU MAKE EIN RESERVATION!

BELLA. *(Very grande dame.)* I have had champagne with pheasant...

CONYERS, GABRIEL & CIRCUS FOLK.
>OOH LA LA LA LA!

>>(*As* **BELLA** *and* **CONYERS** *do a Cossack dance.*)

GABRIEL & CIRCUS FOLK.
>AND SHE HAS HAD VODKA WITH A RUSSIAN PEASANT

BELLA.
>HEY!
>I HAVE KNOWN THE JOYS OF HAVING BACKUP BOYS
>WHO'VE ADORED ME WHILE I'VE TWIRLED

CONYERS & GABRIEL.
>TWIRL, GIRL!

BELLA.

SO EVEN THOUGH AIN'T NO PLACE LIKE HOME
ALL.
IT'S SURE FUN TO ROAM
BELLA.
I LOVE TRAV'LIN' THE WORLD
CONYERS & GABRIEL.
WE LOVE THE LADY STANDING HERE BETWEEN US
BELLA.
TRAV'LIN' THE WORLD
CONYERS & GABRIEL.
THE LOVELY LADY WHO'S A POCKET VENUS
BELLA.
TRAV'LIN' THE WORLD
CONYERS & GABRIEL.
YOU WON'T BE SATISFIED UNTIL YOU'VE SEEN US
BELLA, CONYERS, GABRIEL & CIRCUS FOLK.
TRAV' TRAV' TRAV'LIN'

BELLA.	**CONYERS & GABRIEL.**	**CIRCUS FOLK.**
THE TRAV' TRAV' TRAV'LIN' I LOVE TRAV'LIN'	I WANNA GO TRAV'LIN' TRAV'LIN'	TRAV'LIN' TRAV'LIN'

ALL.
THE WORLD

Scene Twenty-Eight

[MUSIC NO. 20 "MAMA, WHERE DID YOU GO?"]

(**MAMA**'s *back in Tupelo.* **GRANDMA** *has run away.*)

MAMA. Mama please, come out from your hidin' place, now. You hear me? It's time to stop this. I'm sorry I yelled at you, but I swear, Mama, you could try the patience of a saint.

MAMA DONE RUN AWAY
HAD ANOTHER BAD DAY
A BAD DAY YOU CAN'T FACE
SO MAMA FOUND A HIDIN' PLACE
AND AIN'T IT JUST MY LUCK,
YOU DONE SNUCK OUT THE DO'
MAMA, WHERE DID YOU GO?

Mama?

EVEN THOUGH YOU NEED ME
NEVER WANNA HEED ME
YOU MAKE ME HEAVE A SIGH
FEEL LIKE A WASTE OF TIME WHEN I
BE TRYIN' TO MAKE SENSE TO
A MAMA WHO
AIN'T HARDLY THERE NO MO'
MAMA, WHERE DID YOU GO?

OVER AND OVER AND OVER AND OVER AND OVER
WE PLAY THIS LITTLE GAME
AIN'T IT A SHAME
YOU DON'T KNOW YOU PLAYIN'
MAMA, DON'T BE GONE
LET ME KEEP ON, HOLDIN' ON
HOLDIN' ON

> (**AUNT DINAH** *enters with* **GRANDMA**. **MAMA** *rushes to them.*)

You found her.

AUNT DINAH. She was down by the swamp, say she tryin' to get up to the Guntown Depot. Thank the good Lord I got her before anybody could see she was holdin' all that money Bella been sendin' to us right in her hand.

*(***AUNT DINAH** *exits.)*

GRANDMA. They's trouble brewin' on the horizon for my grandbaby, the Itty Bitty Gal done tol' me.

MAMA. All right, Mama, we gonna get to the bottom of it. Now you need to get you some rest –

GRANDMA. But I got to get on that train, Miss Lady, I'm runnin' out of time.

MAMA. Nobody know you runnin' out of time more than me, Mama.

GRANDMA. No, don't you understand I got to go –

MAMA.	**GRANDMA.**
OVER AND OVER	Itty Bitty Gal say Bella 'bout to do
AND OVER AND	something she gonna regret for the rest
OVER AND OVER	of her life if we ain't there to help her
WE PLAY THIS LITTLE GAME	out. She done sent us all that money
AIN'T IT A SHAME	from the circus, there gotta be enough
YOU DON'T KNOW YOU PLAYIN'?	for a train ticket. I got to get on that
	train, I got to go to her –

MAMA.
MAMA, DON'T BE GONE
MAMA, KEEP ON, HOLDIN' ON
HOLDIN' ON

*(***GRANDMA** *puts a loving hand to* **MAMA***'s cheek.)*

GRANDMA. I am holdin' on, daughter.

MAMA. You called me daughter. You know who I am, Mama?

GRANDMA. 'Course I do, baby. You my firstborn. My very own Itty Bitty Gal.

(Suddenly confused.)

Wait a minute, ain't that right?

MAMA. That's right, Mama. I'm your very own Itty Bitty Gal.

(Walking off with her arm around her mother.)

AND THOUGH NOW YOU OKAY
GONNA COME A DAY
WHEN THE THIEF OF TIME
GONNA STEAL YOU AWAY
I HOPE HE FEEL YOUR BITE
WHEN HE TRY TO TAKE YOUR LIGHT
I'LL BE RIGHT BESIDE YOU
GONNA HELP IN THE FIGHT
WITH ALL MY LOVE AND MY CARE
AND THE HELP OF SOME PRAY'R,
MAYBE ONE DAY I'LL KNOW
MAMA, WHERE DID YOU GO?
WHERE DID YOU GO?

Scene Twenty-Nine

(New York City, a concert hall. **CONYERS** *stands in a spotlight.)*

CONYERS. And now, ladies and gentlemen, fresh off of her international tour, for a limited time in Carnegie Hall, the one, the only Bella Patterson –

(**BELLA** *enters.*)

[MUSIC NO. 21 "TRAV'LIN' THE WORLD – REPRISE"]

BELLA.
I WAS NOT THE BEST PUPIL, MY TEACHERS WOULD SAY –

CROWD MEMBER 1. Look at the back staircase on that gal.

(The **CROWD** *laughs, hoots.)*

BELLA.
... NEVER PICKED FOR THE TEAM WHEN MY
SCHOOLMATES WOULD PLAY –

CROWD MEMBER 2. Somebody needs to measure that broad bottom of hers.

CROWD MEMBER 3. It's like there's a haunch of roast beef back there.

BELLA.
BUT I HAD ME THIS BOOK THAT COULD TAKE ME AWAY –

CROWD MEMBER 4. Big booty beauty – more like one of Mother Nature's jokes.

BELLA.	**CROWD.** *(Ad libs.)*
IT WAS ALL ABOUT	Big booty! Show us that ass! Turn around gal, let
TRAV'LIN' THE WORLD	me see what I'm payin' for!

BELLA.
THEY CHEERED FOR ME IN LONDON
THREW FLOWERS AT MY FEET IN ROME
I'M THE BLACK PEARL OF PARIS
AND THIS IS HOW YOU WELCOME ME HOME?

BELLA. The hell with you, then.

(She walks offstage. **GABRIEL** *stops her.)*

GABRIEL. What are you doing? You haven't finished the number.

BELLA. I will not have my talent disparaged by philistines.

GABRIEL. Philistines who are paying five b-bucks a pop.

BELLA. Give them their money back, tell them to spend it on toothpicks for the hayseeds in their teeth. I will not perform for simpletons who don't appreciate my genius.

GABRIEL. Your genius? Nobody's coming here for your genius. They're coming here to l-look at your ass. Oh come on, I tried to keep the worst of the letters away from you, I tried to b-buy up all the papers with the awful cartoons, but surely Bella, you had to know your ass has been the m-main attraction. Now you've got a show to do, so get out there and do it.

BELLA.
BIDE A LITTLE TIME AT THE CIRCUS
WHEN YOU SEE THE MAN-EATING LION –

Ain't no damn lion in this circus – even kitty cats are ashamed to show their faces up in here. Only beast I see is your brother, you know, the one who like to beat up on you and call you an idiot, obviously he know what he's talkin' about.

GABRIEL. D-don't say that, I'm n-not an id-idiot.

BELLA. You one if you think I'ma go back out there.

GABRIEL. There's n-nowhere else for you to g-go.

BELLA. I can go to New Mexico.

GABRIEL. N-no. You can't.

Scene Thirty

(**GABRIEL** *hands her a letter and exits. As* **BELLA** *reads it,* **ALOYSIUS** *enters, seething as he looks at the Big Booty Tupelo Gal poster of* **BELLA**. *He's now in a bar with other* **BUFFALO SOLDIERS**. *He angrily balls up the poster and throws it down, calling out.*)

ALOYSIUS. Bartender.

[MUSIC NO. 22 "DON'T START NO SHIT"]

(*A musical motif is the unseen bartender's surly response. As the motif repeats over and over, the angry* **BUFFALO SOLDIERS** *face the bartender.*)

WHAT DID HE SAY?

SOLDIER 2.

YOU HEARD WHAT HE SAID

SOLDIER 3.

HE SAID, HE DON'T SERVE NO NIGGERS IN HERE

SOLDIER 4. He said, we're lookin' for trouble.

ALOYSIUS. Oh. Are we lookin' for trouble?

SOLDIERS.

NO

ALOYSIUS.

MISTER BARTENDER
WE ONLY COME INTO THIS BAR LOOKIN' FOR A DRINK
WE GOT THE RIGHT TO BE SERVED, NO MATTER WHAT
    YOU THINK
WE GOT THE MONEY, GOT THE THIRST
WE SURE 'NUFF GOT THE GRIT

ALOYSIUS & SOLDIERS.

SO DON'T START NO SHIT
WON'T BE NO SHIT
NO, NO WHOA, WHOA! NO, NO WHOA, WHOA! NO, NO
    WHOA, WHOA!

WE'RE BUFFALO SOLDIERS
THAT'S WHAT THEY CALL US, 'CAUSE WE GOT
THAT THICK AND WOOLLY HAIR
WE GOT THIS TOUGH LEATHER SKIN
WE'RE BROWNER THAN A BEAR
WE BEEN TO HELL, FOUGHT OUR WAY BACK
ACROSS A FIERY PIT
SO DON'T START NO SHIT
WON'T BE NO SHIT

ALOYSIUS.
MY BROTHERS, TESTIFY!

SOLDIER GROUP 1.
WE STRIDE INTO BATTLE
STANDIN' READY AND FORWARD TOGETHER

ALOYSIUS & SOLDIER GROUP 2.
BUFFALO SOLDIERS!

SOLDIER GROUP 1.
BRAVE INDIANS FACE US
WITH WAR PAINT AND PONY AND FEATHER

ALOYSIUS & SOLDIER GROUP 2.
BUFFALO SOLDIERS!

ALOYSIUS.	**GROUP 1.**	**GROUP 2.**
WE FIGHT THE RED MAN AND IT'S DEADLY AND HOT		OOH
BUT THE WHITE MAN'S CONTEMPT IS MUCH COLDER	OOH	OOH
THROUGH FIRE AND ICE WE GIVE IT ALL THAT WE GOT	OOH	OOH
TO EARN THE BUFFALO BADGE ON OUR SHOULDER	OOH	OOH

ALOYSIUS & SOLDIERS.
WE'RE STANDIN' READY AND FORWARD
WE AIN'T STEPPIN' BACK NO MORE!
NO, NO, NO, NO MORE!

SO MISTER BARTENDER
YOU WANNA CALL ME A NIGGER? SAY I'M SECOND CLASS?

> WELL I'M THE NIGGER DEFENDIN' YOUR SORRY WHITE ASS
> NOW PUT THAT BOTTLE ON THE COUNTER LICKETY SPLIT

SOLDIERS.
> DON'T START NO SHIT

ALOYSIUS.
> THAT'S WHAT I WOULD ADVISE

SOLDIERS.
> DON'T START NO SHIT!

ALOYSIUS.
> NO SHIT WHERE SOMEONE DIES

SOLDIERS.
> DON'T START NO SHIT

ALOYSIUS & SOLDIERS.
> YOU BETTER RECOGNIZE THAT
> WE'LL BE FINE
> IF YOU DON'T START NO SHIT!

ALOYSIUS. It's been a struggle to keep my head held high but I'm doin' it, and I won't be drug down by no big booty trash who ain't no better than she oughta be. I'm puttin' you in the past, where all bad memories belong.

> *(He exits. **BELLA** is now in her dressing room. She throws down the letter, collapses on her dressing room couch, grabs a bottle, and starts to drink. Suddenly, **NATHANIEL** breaks through the door.)*

Scene Thirty-One

NATHANIEL. Girl, you hard to get to. Between bribin' the Four Legged Tap Dancer, the Two Headed Nightingale, the Web Footed Duckman and the Tasmanian Wolf Boy, my entire life savin's been cleaned out.

(BELLA runs to him.)

BELLA. Mister Porter? Glory be, you ain't dead.

NATHANIEL. Nah, I ain't dead, just had me a little concussion. Fractured ribs. Broken leg. Black eye. Busted lip. Dizzy spells. Ragin' fever. But I'm fine now, heh, heh, heh.

(Looking around admiringly.)

Hoo whee, you done finally reached that star you been grabbin' for, Miss World Famous Bella Patterson. But why you ain't changed your name? Abolitious okay with that?

BELLA. Who?

NATHANIEL. Abolitious Huckabuck… Alatrocious Huff n' Puff… Ignoramus Humpty Dumpty, you know who I'm talkin' 'bout, the soldier boy.

BELLA. Aloysius Hunnicut. He ain't no concern of mine no more.

NATHANIEL. Ahh. He done give you the mitten, huh? You can't really blame him for leavin' you Bella, you didn't want him anyway. All them stories 'bout people climbin' through train windows for true love and ladies and babies and snakes and spiders, I ain't never heard one time out your mouth any grand romantic tale 'bout Aloysius. Seem to me the only time his name ever come up is when you runnin' away from somethin'. The law. Yourself. Me. Well, I ain't gonna let you run away from me no more. So.

(Getting down on one knee.)

Hold on a second, oh lord got to get down on this busted knee. All right, what do you say? Wanna get hitched?

BELLA. You see these letters here? Every last one of them askin' me that question. I'ma tell you the same thing I tell them – I ain't gonna be your meal ticket or your piece of tail.

NATHANIEL. Don't talk like that –

BELLA. Why not? Everybody else do. Laugh at me like I'm a joke, but the joke's on them, 'cause guess who laughin' all the way to the bank? My daddy died in the war, fightin' for freedom. Or he got killed by a white man who wanted to bed my mama. Or he headed west and never looked back the day Abe Lincoln set him free. Don't matter which of them tall tales is true, the end of the story is, the only one a strong black woman can depend on is herself.

NATHANIEL. I guess that mean you don't want me to get you your stove, huh?

BELLA. My what?

NATHANIEL. I remember a little gal who didn't want nothin' more than a cast-iron coal and wood stove.

BELLA. That gal is gone, Mister Porter. I'm the World Famous Big Booty Gal now, and you ain't nothin' but a man to me.

[MUSIC NO. 23 "NOTHIN' BUT A MAN"]

NATHANIEL.
>LOVELY WOMAN WITH DARK BROWN EYES
>FULL OF MISCHIEF AND SWEET SURPRISE
>GOT A GIGGLE THAT MAKE GREY SKIES TURN BLUE
>
>IF I DREAMT OF A PERFECT MATE
>IF THERE'S ANYONE WORTH THE WAIT
>YOU'RE THAT WOMAN, BUT WHAT AM I TO YOU?
>
>NOTHIN' BUT A MAN
>NOTHIN' BUT A MAN
>NOTHIN' BUT SOME WORD THAT MEAN FALSE HOPE
>AND BITTER DISAPPOINTMENT
>GODDAMNIT BELLA, TELL ME HOW YOU CAN
>LOOK AT ME AND SAY
>I'M NOTHIN' BUT A MAN?

AIN'T NO PICTURE OF TRUE ROMANCE
DON'T LOOK BETTER ON SECOND GLANCE
FURTHEST THING FROM A LUCKY CHANCE COME TRUE
I'M NOTHIN' BUT A MAN
NOTHIN' BUT A MAN
DEALIN' WITH THE TRUMPED UP DECK OF CARDS
MY LIFE DONE DEALT ME
THINKING YOU CARED
I DARED TO SHOW MY HAN'
JUST TO HEAR YOU SAY I'M
NOTHIN' BUT A MAN

SURE AIN'T THE ONE THAT YOU WANTED – HE'S GONE
AND HE LEFT WITHOUT REASON OR RHYME
NOW YOU SAY
ALL BY YOURSELF YOU CAN HAVE A BAD TIME
AIN'T NEVER DONE YOU NO WRONG
STILL YOU ACT LIKE I'M GUILTY OF SOME KIND OF CRIME
BELLA, WHATCHA THINKIN' OF ME?

DO YOU HATE ME?
... COULD YOU LOVE ME?

    (**BELLA** *gives him a blank stare.*)

... COOL AND DISTANT BEHIND YOUR MASK
GETTIN' THROUGH IS A USELESS TASK
WON'T REPLY TO NO QUESTIONS I ASK

SO IT ENDS TODAY
TIME TO WALK AWAY
HEADIN' FOR THE DOOZY OF A JOKE I CALL MY FUTURE
FAR FROM THE MEM'RY THAT I LEAVE BEHIN'
THE MEM'RY OF A HEART
SOARIN' WITH THE BIRDS
SHOT DOWN BY YOUR WORDS
NOTHIN', NOTHIN'
I'M NOTHIN' BUT A MAN

Not that it matter to you, but my name is Beckworth. Nathaniel Beckworth. Goodbye, Bella.

Scene Thirty-Two

(**BELLA** *reaches out for* **NATHANIEL**, *but it's too late: he's gone. She reaches for her bottle again, but it's now empty. She opens a drawer, pulls out another bottle, it's also empty. She scrabbles around in the drawer, pulls out a vial of liquid, opens it, pours it into a shot glass. As she puts the glass to her lips, the* **SPIRIT OF THE BOOTY** *appears in the mirror.*)

SPIRIT OF THE BOOTY. Once you start that up, gonna be hard to stop.

BELLA. What are you doin' here?

SPIRIT OF THE BOOTY. Don't you remember? I come to you in times of crisis.

BELLA. This ain't no crisis, it's just somethin' to get me through this night.

SPIRIT OF THE BOOTY. Mm, mm, mm. Man took a bullet for you, bounced with you down a mountain, tracked you down to make sure you was okay. But you just gonna give him up and drown yourself in drink and dope. You got a problem, gal.

[MUSIC NO. 24 "YOU DON'T KNOW WHAT YA GOT UNTIL IT'S GONE"]

BELLA. And here's what it is.
I'M SICK OF BEIN' THE LIFE OF SOMEONE'S PARTY
WHERE I DON'T GET TO HAVE NO PIECE OF CAKE!
I'M SICK OF ENTERTAININ' FOLKS
WHO MAKIN' ME THE BUTT OF JOKES
WHO ACT LIKE I AIN'T GOT A HEART TO BREAK!
I'M SICK OF HOW THEY LOOK AT ME
BECAUSE THE ONLY THING THEY SEE IS YOU
... AND SUDDENLY, I KNOW JUST WHAT TO DO...

(*She starts grabbing her behind, trying to wrench it off.*)

SPIRIT OF THE BOOTY. *(Grimacing in pain.)* Ow, stop it, what are you doin'?

BELLA. Gettin' rid of you.

SPIRIT OF THE BOOTY. You can't get rid of a big booty.

BELLA. And yet I'm –

> *(She wrenches it off.)*

– doin' it.

> *(She marches out of the room, the **SPIRIT OF THE BOOTY** trailing her.)*

SPIRIT OF THE BOOTY. You're makin' a mistake.

> YOU DON'T KNOW WHAT YA GOT UNTIL IT'S GONE!

I saved you when you fell off that roof, tryin' to grab for the star, when that awful man tried to have his way with you, when the train got robbed, when you crashed down the mountainside. Even in this circus, I'm your biggest asset.

> YOU DON'T KNOW WHAT YA GOT UNTIL IT'S GONE
> LIKE A JOB WITH A COMFORTABLE WAGE
> LIKE THE HAIR ON YOUR HEAD
> WHEN YOU REACH MIDDLE AGE
> LIKE THE BOOTY THAT YOU GIVE UP
> 'CAUSE YOU BLINDED WITH RAGE
> YOU DON'T KNOW WHAT YA GOT UNTIL IT'S GONE

Where you goin' with me?

BELLA. Isn't it obvious? I'm throwing you over the cliffs.

> *(During the following, there is a cacophony of horns honking, horses whinnying, screams and shouts at the sight of **BELLA** toting her behind to New Jersey on the Weehawken Ferry.)*

SPIRIT OF THE BOOTY. Those cliffs in New Jersey? By the Hudson River? You couldn't – you wouldn't –

BELLA. I'm gonna be booty-free at last.

SPIRIT OF THE BOOTY. Bella, don't act hasty.

> YOU DON'T KNOW WHAT YA GOT UNTIL –

BELLA.
>YOU CAN BEG YOU CAN PLEAD
>I AIN'T PAYIN' YOU NO HEED
>SO TALK ON AND ON
>AIN'T NOTHIN' YOU CAN SAY GONNA CHANGE MY MIND

SPIRIT OF THE BOOTY.
>YOU DON'T KNOW WHAT YA GOT UNTIL IT'S GONE
>BETTER LISTEN GIRL, YOU BEEN DULY WARNED
>WHAT YOU DOIN'S TOO IMPULSIVE
>
>AND YA KNOW I'LL BE MOURNED
>I'M LIKE THE HIST'RY OF YOUR PEOPLE
>DON'T LET HIST'RY BE SCORNED
>'CAUSE YOU DON'T KNOW WHAT YA GOT UNTIL IT'S GONE

>*(In desperation, as **BELLA** arrives at the cliffs.)*
>
>I NEED SOME HELP NOW

SPIRITS OF SOME BODY.
>SOME HELP

SPIRIT OF THE BOOTY.
>FROM SOMEBODY, OR PARTS OF SOME BODY

SPIRITS OF SOME BODY.
>HERE WE ARE

>*(Astral projections indicate the presence of the **SPIRITS OF SOME BODY**.)*

SPIRIT OF THE NOSE. We have been sent to you by the spirit of the Itty Bitty Gal. We are the language of your nose.

SPIRIT OF THE LIPS. And lips.

SPIRIT OF THE HAIR. And hair.

SPIRIT OF THE LEGS. And legs.

SPIRIT OF THE FEET. And feet.

SPIRIT OF THE THIGHS. And thighs.

SPIRIT OF THE HAIR. We have come to tell you to hold onto what makes you unique, Bella.

SPIRIT OF THE LEGS. You must do this.

SPIRIT OF THE LIPS. For all the girls who came before you.

SPIRIT OF THE HAIR. And for all those who will follow you.

SPIRITS OF SOME BODY.	**SPIRIT OF THE BOOTY.**
'CAUSE LIKE THE LEAVES ON THE TREES AT THE END OF THE YEAR	YOU DON'T KNOW
LIKE THE LIFE THAT GETS WASTED BY HATRED AND FEAR	YOU DON'T KNOW, NO!
LIKE THE POWERS THAT HELP YOU, BUT SOON DISAPPEAR YOU DON'T KNOW WHAT YOU GOT UNTIL IT'S –	NO! NO! NO! NO!

  (**BELLA** *tosses her booty over the cliff.*)

SPIRIT OF THE BOOTY.
 NO!
SPIRITS OF THE BODY.
 GONE

Scene Thirty-Three

(TOMMIE HAW enters.)

TOMMIE. You gonna throw us away, too?

BELLA. Tommie Haw.

(As all the characters from her train ride enter.)

And Ida Lou, the lady with the baby. Diego. Miss Cabbagestalk. Snaggletooth. I didn't think I'd never see y'all again. I ain't seein' you now, am I? No – you just my wild imagination.

MISS CABBAGESTALK. You say that like a wild imagination is a bad thing.

BELLA. Well, what on earth is it good for?

DIEGO. Encontrando color glorioso en un mundo que es aburrido y gris.

MISS CABBAGESTALK. He said, finding glorious color in a world that's dull and grey –

BELLA. Girl, I speak Spanish in my imagination.

SNAGGLETOOTH. Well, you just imagined yourself out of one of your best attributes, and I'll be a hornswogglin' monkey's uncle, if I can figure out how the heck you're s'posed come to the end of this here adventure without your end.

TOMMIE. 'Cause gettin' that fine, fine backside back is gonna be impossible, Bella.

ALL. Impossible.

BELLA. Impossible?

[MUSIC NO. 25 "IMPOSSIBLE"]

I STOPPED ME A ROBBER FROM ROBBIN' A TRAIN
I BOUNCED DOWN A MOUNTAIN WITHOUT TOO MUCH PAIN
I'M BLACK, I'M A WOMAN, AND I AIN'T INSANE
NOW *THAT'S* WHAT'S IMPOSSIBLE!

I NAVIGATE A WORLD OF DANGER
WITH EACH AND EV'RY BREATH THAT I TAKE
SO CLIMBIN' DOWN A SLIPP'RY SLOPE
WITHOUT NO TRAIL, WITHOUT NO ROPE
WITHOUT NO HOPE HAS GOTTA BE A PIECE OF CAKE!

DIDN'T THINK MY UNIQUENESS
WAS WORTH MY RESPECT
I MISTOOK MY STRENGTH FOR WEAKNESS
MY SOUL I DID REJECT
WITH THESE PEARLS OF NEW-FOUND WISDOM
MY LIFE WILL BE BEDECKED
THAT'S HOW I WILL FACE THE IMPOSSIBLE

SO, IF THE STORMS OF LIFE SHOULD RAGE AND BELLOW
AND IF THE BEST OF TIMES SHOULD BE THE WORST
I AM GONNA SOLDIER ON, ALL THE SAME
NOTHIN' EVER, EVER GONNA QUENCH MY FLAME
IF YA WANNA BEAT ME AT MY GAME
YA GOTTA CATCH ME FIRST

I FEEL THE VOICES OF MY ANCESTORS WRAPPIN' AROUND ME

BELLA & TRAIN CHARACTERS.
FORGOTTEN SOULS
UNWRITTEN PAGES
SPANNING THE AGES
IN UNSEEN GLORY
REVEALING MY STORY

BELLA.	**TRAIN CHARACTERS.**
I'M DONE FENCIN' WITH A SWORD	WE ARE THE VOICES
HANGIN' OVER MY HEAD	OF YOUR ANCESTORS
I'M DONE SWALLOWIN' WHOLE	WRAPPIN' AROUND YOU
EV'RY LIE I BEEN FED	FORGOTTEN SOULS
AIN'T GONNA LIE DOWN	UNWRITTEN PAGES
AND TAKE IT NO MORE	

BELLA.	TRAIN CHARACTERS 1.	TRAIN CHARACTERS 2.
JUST 'CAUSE SOMEBODY SAY I MADE MY BED	SPANNING THE AGES	NOTHING'S IMPOSSIBLE!
Y'ALL, I'M 'BOUT TO TURN IT ON ITS HEAD	IN UNSEEN GLORY	NOTHING'S IMPOSSIBLE!

BELLA & TRAIN CHARACTERS.
'CAUSE NOTHIN' IS IMPOSSIBLE!

(**BELLA** *yells out on the top of the cliffs.*)

BELLA. I am Bella Patterson, The Big Booty Tupelo Gal. And I'm lettin' the whole world know
I WANT MY BOOTY BACK!

TRAIN CHARACTERS.
HALLELUJAH, BELLA WANTS HER BOOTY BACK!

BELLA.
I NEED MY BOOTY BACK!

TRAIN CHARACTERS.
HALLELUJAH, BELLA NEEDS HER BOOTY BACK!

BELLA.
I'LL GET MY BOOTY BACK!

TRAIN CHARACTERS.
HALLELUJAH
BELLA'S GONNA GET HER BOOTY BACK!
SHE'S GONNA DO THE IMPOSSIBLE

BELLA.
I'M GONNA CLIMB ON DOWN THIS MOUNTAIN
I'M GONNA FORGE A BRAND NEW TRAIL
AND I KNOW I'M PROB'LY GONNA STUMBLE
AND IT'S LIKELY I'M GONNA FAIL
BUT MY FAILURE AIN'T GONNA BE FINAL
I'M GONNA LEARN FROM MY MISTAKES
'CAUSE THAT'S WHAT IT TAKES TO ACHIEVE THE IMPOSSIBLE

TRAIN CHARACTERS.
IMPOSSIBLE, IMPOSSIBLE, IMPOSSIBLE, IMPOSSIBLE!

BELLA.	**TRAIN CHARACTERS.**
IMPOSSIBLE AIN'T NOTHIN' BUT A BIG WORD	AHHH
KEEP TELLIN' ME I SHOULDN'T EVEN TRY	AHHH, AHHH
TELLIN' ME I BETTER KNOW MY PLACE	
BUT I'M GONNA MEET IT FACE TO FACE	
THEN I'M GONNA SMILE AT IT, MIGHT EVEN WINK MY EYE	
THEN I'M GONNA KISS "IMPOSSIBLE" GOOD-BYE	

[MUSIC NO. 26 "THE RETURN OF BONNY JOHNNY – REPRISE"]

*(The characters – all except for **SNAGGLETOOTH**, who has exited – applaud **BELLA**. The **SNAGGLETOOTH** actor re-enters, now as **BONNY JOHNNY RAKEHELL**. As all the characters stare at him.)*

TOMMIE HAW. Who the hell is that?

JOHNNY. I'm Bonny Johnny Rakehell the beau of Chickasaw, although I come from way down south –

BELLA. Blah, BLAH, blah, BLAH, blah, BLAH.

JOHNNY. *(Temper tantrum.)* No, no, no, no, you blithering idiot. I'm Bonny Johnny Rakehell the beau of Chickasaw, although I come from way down south, I live –

BELLA. Blah, BLAH, blah, BLAH.

JOHNNY. Above the law –

BELLA. Blah, BLAH, blah, BLAH.

JOHNNY. I live above the –

BELLA. Blah, BLAH, blah, BLAH.

>   (**JOHNNY** *furiously stomps his feet.*)

JOHNNY. I live above the law, I live above the law, I live above the –

>   (*His stomping causes him to trip and fall off the cliff, yelling.*)

LAWWWWWWWWWWW –

>   (**BELLA** *looking over the edge.*)

BELLA. Not any more, you don't.

Scene Thirty-Four

> (**GRANDMA** *enters on the arm of* **NATHANIEL**. *She's holding* **BELLA**'s *booty.*)

BELLA. Grandma, what you doin' here?

GRANDMA. Itty Bitty Gal came to me in a dream, say, go forth to New Jersey and make sure at least one black woman in this world get a happy endin' to her story. And speakin' of a happy end, what *you* doin' throwin' this booty away?

> (*As the* **TRAIN CHARACTERS** *reattach* **BELLA**'s *booty.*)

BELLA. How'd you find it?

GRANDMA. I told you, Itty Bitty Gal guide me to it. Guide me to this nice young man, too. He a Pullman Porter, and his name –

BELLA. Is Nathaniel Beckworth, and he the best thing in the world ever happen to me, and if he still wanna know what my dream is, it's that I hope he forgive me. Can you do that, Nathaniel?

> (**NATHANIEL** *thinks about it. Then:*)

NATHANIEL. No.

> (**GRANDMA** *tries to smooth out the awkward pause*)

GRANDMA. … Okay…well, uh…thanks for helping me up the mountain anyway.

> (**NATHANIEL** *kisses* **GRANDMA**'s *hand.*)

NATHANIEL. My pleasure ma'am. Good day to you.

> (*He starts to exit.*)

BELLA. Nathaniel Beckworth, you stop right there. Now you listen to me.

[MUSIC NO. 27 "WHAT I WANT / GAL OVER YONDER – REPRISE"]

BELLA.
>I WANT A PHILO STEWART CAST-IRON COAL AND WOOD STOVE

NATHANIEL. What you want that for?

BELLA. So I can cook me up some food for the man I love. That would be you.

NATHANIEL. What kind of food?

BELLA. Hoppin' John.

NATHANIEL. Hoppin' John and sweet potato pie?

BELLA. If that's what you want.

NATHANIEL. Oh yeah,
>THAT IS WHAT I WANT

BELLA.
>THEN COME HERE LITTLE BOY, COME AND TAKE MY HAND
>I'M YOUR LOVE FOREVERLASTIN'

NATHANIEL.
>YOUR LOVE FOREVERLASTIN'

MAMA. You think he's gonna marry her?

GRANDMA. He done seen my grandbaby naked ass, hell yeah, he gonna marry her.

BELLA & NATHANIEL.
>I'M YOUR LOVE FOREVERLASTIN' BEAU

>*(They kiss.)*

Scene Thirty-Five

[MUSIC NO. 28 "BIG BOOTY TUPELO GAL - REPRISE"]

(**BELLA** *steps out of the scene.*)

BELLA. *(In her **NARRATOR** role.)*

SOME FOLKS ARE SCANDALIZED BY THE FAME OF HER
SOME PEOPLE FAINT AT THE NAME OF HER
BUT IT'S A MYSTERY WHAT BECAME OF HER

It really wasn't a mystery. The simple fact of the matter was that Bella had been left out of the history books. But as you can see, it ain't that easy to get rid of a big booty. Just keep poppin' up when you least expect it. Her grandma said it best when she said,

GRANDMA. Make your memory so big, nobody ever forget.

(*As all the characters from the story enter.*)

BELLA. And after all, what are we but our memories?

BELLA.	**ALL.**
So remember, ladies and gentlemen:	OOOO

ALL.

HISTORY IS THE TALL TALE
THAT YOU LEARN FROM THE BOOK OF THE SCHOLAR
BUT THERE'S ANOTHER HISTORY
YOU CAN LEARN FROM THE TALE THAT IS TALLER

(**BELLA** *holds up a dime store novel.*)

BELLA. And this one is available right out there in the lobby, two for one, get 'em while they last. *The Thrillin' Adventures of Tupelo Bella.*

ALL EXCEPT BELLA.

NOW DON'T YOU FORGET IT
'CAUSE IT'S YOUR STORY, TOO

BELLA.

AND I SWEAR, IT'S ONE HUNDRED AND TEN PERCENT
ABSOLUTELY TRUE!

End of Show

www.ingramcontent.com/pod-product-compliance
Lightning Source LLC
Chambersburg PA
CBHW051404290426
44108CB00015B/2154